What People Are Saying About *Read for Your Life*

"I learned at an early age the importance of good books for personal growth. Regular reading has been a personal discipline I've practiced for over four decades. No matter where you want to go in life, reading the right books will help you get there. Pat Williams's book *Read for Your Life* will help you learn how to make the most of your reading experience."

—**John C. Maxwell**, *New York Times* bestselling author

"Reading is the skill that makes life magnificent, enjoyable, adventurous, and enchanted. I invite you to become a great and inspired reader by drinking in the wisdom of my brilliant and funny friend, Pat Williams."

—**Mark Victor Hansen**, cocreator, #1 *New York Times* bestselling
Chicken Soup for the Soul series cocreator, *Cracking the Millionaire
Code* and *The One Minute Millionaire*

"Pat Williams has finally used everything I taught him about writing and has produced a book a writer *has to* endorse. Don't miss this one."

—**Jerry B. Jenkins**, bestselling author of the Left Behind series

"Pat Williams has a magical way to capture the imaginations of his readers. He wields that magic in his latest work, *Read for Your Life*. You will enjoy the various facets he explores. Pat is awesome, baby!"

—**Dick Vitale**, ESPN college basketball analyst and sports celebrity

"If your eyes are up to it, then read *Read for Your Life*, because it goes from your eyes to your heart and your brain and your funny bone to your loneliness, and perhaps even to your conscience. Read it!"

—**Mike Wallace**, former *60 Minutes* journalist and CBS News
correspondent emeritus

"I grew up in a reading family, but until I read Pat Williams's new book I never realized how important reading is to every area of our lives. Very few books are life-changers, but this one is."

—**Grant Hill**, Orlando Magic superstar

"As Pat Williams suggests, reading is as necessary as air to the examined life. Where else or how else can you traverse the woods with the *Deerslayer,* sail with Jack London, and pitch for the Yankees without leaving your pillow? Reading is your ticket everywhere."

—**Mike Veeck**, Marketing wizard and baseball owner and consultant

"As the old saying goes, 'Leaders are readers.' Pat Williams makes that abundantly clear in his encouraging new book, *Read for Your Life*. After reading these pages, I guarantee you'll become a more inspired and motivated reader—and leader."

—**Ken Blanchard**, Coauthor of *The One Minute Manager* and *Leading at a Higher Level*

"Anything that strengthens reading strengthens our country. I'm for that, and if this book creates one more reader, then it deserves our praise."

—**Ken Burns**, legendary documentary filmmaker

"I am a lover of books, and this project by Pat Williams is a great one. This wonderful, warm, witty book instructs and inspires you to be a better, more avid reader all of your life."

—**Brian Tracy**, author of *The Power of Charm*

"Not many people could make reading sound "magical," but Pat Williams has. I'm going to get this book in every parent's hands I know to make sure they get the message."

—**Brian Kilmeade**, cohost of *Fox & Friends in the Morning* and author of *The Games Do Count*

"In a time when machines are taking over the world, Pat Williams explains to kids why they must read to succeed. Parents, use that rhyme and buy Pat's book for your children."

—**Bill O'Reilly**, anchor, Fox News Channel

"A terrific book. An important book. One that should be read by every parent, especially those with young children."

—**Warren Bennis**, Distinguished Professor of Business, University of Southern California, and author of *On Becoming a Leader*

"Pat Williams is a very successful author, having authored forty-plus books, but this one, *Read for Your Life*, is his best and will have a positive impact on your life."

—**Lou Holtz**, former University of Notre Dame Head Coach and college football personality

READ
FOR YOUR
LIFE

11 Ways to Transform Your
Life with Books

PAT WILLIAMS
with Peggy Matthews Rose

Health Communications, Inc.
Deerfield Beach, Florida

www.hcibooks.com

Library of Congress Cataloging-in-Publication Data

Williams, Pat.
  Read for your life : 11 ways to transform your life with books / Pat
Williams with Peggy Matthews Rose.
      p.   cm.
  Includes bibliographical references (p.) and index.
  ISBN-13: 978-0-7573-0545-0 (trade paper)
  ISBN-10: 0-7573-0545-8 (trade paper)
    1. Reading promotion—United States. 2. Books and reading—
United States. I. Rose, Peggy Matthews. II. Title.
  Z1003.2.W56 2007
  028'.9—dc22
                                                            2006103117

Publisher: Health Communications, Inc.
            3201 S.W. 15th Street
            Deerfield Beach, FL 33442-8190

Cover photo © JupiterImages
Cover and interior design by Lawna Patterson Oldfield

To David Stern,
Commissioner of the National
Basketball Association, whose commitment
to the NBA's Read to Achieve
program has impacted thousands
of young lives.

—Pat Williams

In memory of my mother,
Helen Matthews, who taught me
to love words and books, to wield a pencil
at a young age, and let me crowd her
into a kitchen corner while I read
her everything I wrote.

—Peggy Matthews Rose

Contents

Foreword

I grew up in a reading home. My mom, as moms will do, had a huge influence on me. Mom was a regular reader, and our house was constantly filled with books on a wide variety of topics. My mother influenced me to start reading when I was five years old. She would tape Scriptures to the wall for us to memorize. In our house, we had the Bible—and we had books about the Bible. That's what I read. Then we got a set of the *World Book Encyclopedia*, and I read every volume.

That love of reading Mom inspired has only grown over the years. It may sound strange to some of you that a man who's made his living in the world of professional sports would be an avid reader, but today my love of reading is a secret to no one. In fact, I'm pretty well known for putting appropriate books in the hands of all my NBA players. I'm a strong believer in reading, and, whenever I can, I am front and center on the importance of reading. I'm glad to have had a part in improving the lives of those under my leadership.

When my friend Pat Williams told me he was working on a book about reading, I was excited! And then I thought, *Pat, who's going to read a book about reading? People who don't read—are they going to read it? And people who do read—why would they read it?*

But as I read through the manuscript, I really changed my mind. I had never considered all the benefits of reading—like the fact that it's a safeguard against old age, or that it makes you the most interesting person at the dinner table. Reading makes your mind sharp, alive, vibrant. It keeps you on the cutting edge. Like a healthy body, a healthy mind is honed like a razor. And it's reading that does that—nothing else! Not television, not movies, not playing golf—not even shooting hoops. This book will inspire you to view reading as one of the essentials of your life—which it is—like eating, sleeping, and exercising. It is *not* an option.

I've often expressed my belief that teamwork is the art of selflessness. Reading appears to be an act of self-satisfaction, but ultimately it is a selfless endeavor. When we read, we become more interesting people. We become team players in the game of life, people with whom others want to engage. Books fill our minds with ideas and information we can pass on to others. When we read, we become excited about reading, and we can't wait to share our current favorite or just get others excited about reading, too.

I have a practical rule for my teams: when the ball comes into your hands and you hold it for longer than two counts, you've destroyed the team's rhythm. When you hold the ball, all eyes are on you. And when *you* become the focus, the system breaks down.

I believe it's that way with books, too. We have a responsibility not to let the knowledge we gain from books be put on hold in our minds. Pat Williams has done a wonderful job of making that point in *Read for Your Life*. If we don't learn from what others have passed on to us, and then pass on what we've learned to others, our system breaks down, just as it does on the basketball court. It's critical we not let that happen. "Game over" is not a term we want to become our literacy legacy. I know I don't, and I don't think you do, either.

Rick Warren reports that half the world is illiterate. That's a global crisis! We've got to help solve it. *Read for Your Life* can be a wonderful starting point. After reviewing *Read for Your Life*, I am more sold on reading than ever. This book reinforces the truth that reading is not about you alone, and I truly appreciate that. Instead of giving my players one book to read, I may start giving them two—including this one!

Phil Jackson, Head Coach, Los Angeles Lakers

Acknowledgments

With deep appreciation I acknowledge the support and guidance of the following people who helped make this book possible:

Special thanks to Bob Vander Weide and Rich DeVos of the Orlando Magic.

I'm grateful to my assistant, Andrew Herdliska, who managed so many details that made this book possible. Thanks also to my writing partner, Peggy Matthews Rose, for her superb contributions in shaping this manuscript.

Hats off to four dependable associates—my longtime adviser Ken Hussar, my ace typist Fran Thomas, and coworkers Latria Graham and Jennica Pearson.

Hearty thanks also go to my friend Peter Vegso and his capable staff at Health Communications, Inc. Thank you all for believing that we had something important to share, and for providing the support and the forum to say it.

And, finally, special thanks and appreciation go to my wife, Ruth, and to my wonderful and supportive family. They are truly the backbone of my life.

Read for Your Life Way No. 1:

Get Over the *Fear* Factor

Introduction: The Trouble with Reading

We live in one of the greatest eras of communication known to man, yet nearly every day, somewhere in America, headlines spell out the news that reading, as a skill, is dying. I don't know about you, but that fact alarms me . . . and it's the reason I've written this book. As you engage in conversation with me through these pages, please think hard about your own future, your children's future, and our nation's future. I believe that much is at stake.

To most of the outside world, I'm known as a basketball executive. Sports, from baseball to the NBA, have written most of my life story. But behind the scenes—and sometimes right there on the court—I'm a reader. Books are my passion. I love to learn. So when I hear that reading is in trouble, I get riled.

This isn't the first time in history that books have been imperiled, but if you'll hang with me over these next few pages and be willing to see the role you're meant to play, I hope that, together, we can make it the last. I believe it is one of our greatest challenges.

Warning Signs We May Have Missed

In a world where few people read, the vast stores of knowledge found in books are either lost or reside with a select few. Is that the future we want?

In the early to mid-twentieth century, several popular novels foretold a possible future without books. One of the best known, and still widely read, is Ray Bradbury's *Fahrenheit 451*. When this classic was first published back in 1953, the idea that all books would one day be banned was pretty startling. The novel's main character is a fireman—but not the type of fireman who would rescue us from a burning building. Bradbury's fireman burns books. At one point, the protagonist, fireman Guy Montag, asks Fire Chief Beatty what started it all. Deep down, this job he'd simply done for so long was beginning to trouble him. *Why* did they burn books?

In Bradbury's imaginary future, books were banned by government edict. It's certainly happened before, in various dark corners of the world where repressive regimes banned or burned books. Aldous Huxley's *Brave New World,* which debuted in 1932, also suggested a world without books. His ideas, however, might have been closer to the picture today's headlines spell out. Huxley suggested a world without books simply because people no longer cared about reading or bothered to learn.

Where one begins by burning books,
one will end up burning people.

—Heinrich Heine, eighteenth-century German poet

What About You?

So let me ask you—are you a reader? I don't mean, *can* you read? (By the way, if you can, you are in the minority compared with the world's population, so be thankful.) No, I'm not asking if you *can* read, but if you *do* read. Do you love books? Are books part of your day, every day? If not, why not? Mark Twain is often quoted as observing, "A person who won't read has no advantage over one who can't read." If you are not a regular reader, then *you* are currently part of the problem.

If you love books, as I do, ask what you and I can do to turn back the pages, as it were, to a time when reading was a prime-time activity. Ask yourself what you can do to keep the future, fictionalized by Bradbury and Huxley, from becoming fact. Be part of the solution. You can thank me for it later.

In this book, I challenge you to examine your own reading habits and those of your household, circle of friends, and community. I hope to inspire you to improve your own reading habits and then pass that passion on to those you love before you leave this world. Books can take you places you'd never get to otherwise. Come along with me; let me show you how.

1

The Startling Truth
About Tomorrow

In the summer of 2004, *Newsweek* ran an article based on a study released that year by the National Endowment for the Arts (NEA). According to the article, reading in America is on the decline as people turn more and more to electronic forms of entertainment and communication. At one time, young adults, aged eighteen to thirty-four, were the most active readers in the land. But since 1982, that number has dropped by a stunning 28 percent, making this group now the *least* active in terms of reading.

According to the NEA report, "at the current rate of loss, literary reading as a leisure activity will virtually disappear in half a century." Ray Bradbury saw this potential reality a half-century ago! It was a scene from a science-fiction novel then, but today, in this first decade of the twenty-first century, it's closer to becoming fact. I submit, however, that it's not, as *Fahrenheit 451* suggests, a result of overpopulation. Rather, we are in danger of losing our very souls—that part of us that actively engages with the hearts and minds of others, the part that lives on into eternity, reaches across time, and spans the generations—due to *preoccupation*.

What we become depends on what
we read after all of the professors have
finished with us. The greatest university
of all is a collection of books.

—Thomas Carlyle, nineteenth-century writer and journalist

Watching Is Not Reading

Ever since movie producers began putting classic stories on the screen, students have preferred "the movie version" when it comes to book reports. This is not a new phenomenon—we were pulling this trick when I was in school. These condensed adaptations are much easier for the lazy-minded who just want to "get through" class. But today, many kids don't even bother with the movie. They simply come home, turn on the TV, and zone out.

In their book *Shelf Life,* Dr. George Grant, director of the Kings Meadow Study Center in Tennessee, and his wife, Karen, cite author Richard Hoggart's opinion that we live in a "postliterate" society. "Television," they wrote, "is America's drug of choice—a kind of electronic Valium."

As if to underscore that comment, an August 2006 Associated Press article by Seth Borenstein reported research that found television literally has a numbing effect. Hospital-conducted research has concluded that children distracted by TV are less aware of receiving shots.

Bob Orben, an author who specializes in books for speakers, has observed: "Young people today are as bright and quick and potentially teachable as ever. The problem is they are no longer readers. They are watchers. Their most influential classroom is the TV screen. With each passing year, they know less and less about more and more."

*Reading seems like such a simple
skill, but it holds back many people in college.
Once you can read competently, you have a
chance to be educated, but not until.*

—John McKay, former head football coach,
University of Southern California and Tampa Bay Buccaneers

President George W. Bush reminds us that, in order for future educational forecasts to change, we parents must pay closer attention to what our children are doing after school. "We cannot blame the schools alone for the dismal decline in SAT verbal scores," he said. "When our kids come home from school, do they pick up a book, or do they sit glued to the tube, watching music videos? Parents, don't make the mistake of thinking your kid only learns between 9 AM and 3 PM."

I could not agree more with these experts. Television is addictive. Watch a youngster sometime when he or she is tuned in to a favorite show. Everything else is tuned out. Their eyes glaze over. They're mesmerized! Television carries with it a mentality that says, "Entertain me. Make it easy for me." Reading says, "Challenge me. Stimulate me. Push my mind. Make it work. Make me think."

I'm not saying television has no value. Television is one of the marvels of the twentieth century! In my book on Walt Disney (*How to Be Like Walt,* HCI, 2004), we met Philo T. Farnsworth, who, in 1927, filed a patent for an invention called the television. He named it for a fictional device he'd read about in the *Amazing Stories* science-fiction magazine.

When young Farnsworth saw the first image on his screen—Walt Disney's *Steamboat Willy,* transmitted just two years after filing his patent—I'm sure he saw it as a tool that would enrich Americans and eventually all the people in the world. And truthfully, it does. Television is a wonderful thing!

Because of TV, viewers can sit at home and watch sporting events, concerts, documentaries, and more. But they can also waste a lot of time watching junk—and many of them do. Television is an amazing tool, but it could do so much more. You and I both know that. As former FCC commissioner Nicholas Johnson said, "All television is educational television. The question is: what is it teaching?"

Books Need to Be First Choice

En route to a speaking engagement in Atlanta not long ago, I argued briefly with myself over the need to purchase a copy of the *Atlanta Journal-Constitution*, then plunked down my fifty cents. Who would have guessed I would find in its pages an editorial aimed directly at the problem with reading in America? But there it was, right before my eyes. Louisiana writer Jennifer Moses captured my heart on this vital issue. "Today's high-school graduates are more poorly equipped for college than students of previous generations," she wrote, "and the reason is simple: they don't read. It's not that they can't read, mind you—Americans on the whole are the most literate society on the face of the Earth, with illiteracy rates steadily dropping.

"But today's students—like their elders—are in the grip of what I call post-literacy. True, they have board scores that would make Einstein weep with envy, varsity letters, and experience digging drainage ditches in the Third World—not to mention perfect grades and teeth—but without having put in the time snuggling up with a good book, they're intellectually handicapped" (May 15, 2006).

Moses cites as a source of her information a university professional who said that, while students' test scores and GPAs are higher than ever, they are less prepared for college. He faults the huge amount of information they are bombarded with, along with the way in which they are being taught.

*Not only have we failed to close the
achievement gap between rich and poor, and
between minorities and whites, but our young
people now face growing pressure from Asian
students hungry for a better life. "When I compare
our high schools to what I see when I'm traveling
abroad," said Bill Gates, "I am terrified
for our workforce of tomorrow."*

—David Gergen, "The Danger of Drift,"
U.S. News & World Report (May 29, 2006)

"It's almost as if," Moses writes, "with our reliance on the
Internet and other technological sources of information, students are only able to digest information in tiny, fragmentary
bits . . .

"Cultural mirrors aside, what's really troubling about post-
literacy isn't that too few people delve into complex works of
history, economics, biography, or literature—not to mention
know how to recite the prologue to *The Canterbury Tales,* parse
a Shakespearean sonnet, or tackle the later works of Henry
James—but rather, that we, as a nation of citizens, are letting our
brains turn into big, soggy masses of gray goop. When your brains
turn to mush, it's hard to tease out meaning or discern hard and
often-ugly facts amid mountains of spin and image-making."

That's a pretty frightening picture, but I believe Ms. Moses is
right. If we don't get a handle on this problem soon, our future
ability even to think is at stake!

Instead of wasting time on mindless pursuits or frantically
striving to keep up with a world moving at warp speed, read a
book—and learn something! Feed your mind. Yes, we all need to

relax our minds from time to time—I'm not suggesting we don't—but think how much better off you might be if you rested by feeding your mind new thoughts from a book, rather than watching the latest episode of a TV series that will be canceled and forgotten faster than you can say "Philo T. Farnsworth."

In the early years of television, it was even hoped that the attention children gave to TV would improve their interest in reading. Indeed, it might have if TV, left to itself, consisted of uninterrupted narratives . . . If we want to have the best of all possible worlds, we had better realize that we cannot have all the worlds. I believe that television commercials have got to go.

—Norman Mailer, author

Writer Charley Reese, formerly of the *Orlando Sentinel,* observed, "I feel sorry for people who grow up not liking to read, as apparently more and more young Americans are doing. They are inadvertently shortening . . . their lives. Not physically, of course, but the life of a human is essentially the life of the mind. With good books, you can live several thousand years in the short physical span you have, and you can live a life far more rich in experience than all but the most heroic adventures . . . Nothing in my life was so fortuitous as falling in love with books at an early age . . . You don't have to wait for medical breakthroughs to extend your life and the richness of it. All you need are a library card, the knowledge of how to read in your native language, and a desire not to be bled to death by commercial vampires who trade junk for pieces of your precious life."

Charley understands the problem.

In her book *The Funny Pages,* author Judy Brown cites this comment from comedian Lily Tomlin, "If you read a lot of books, you're considered well-read, but if you watch a lot of TV, you're not considered well-viewed."

Between television, movies, video games, cell phones, work, Internet surfing, e-mail, chat rooms, and blogging, most of us spend little time between the old-fashioned covers of an actual, hold-in-your-hands book nowadays. This applies especially to young people in America—and particularly to males! Fellas, I'm sorry if the truth hurts, but we've got to face up to it!

In an article for the *Writer's Digest* website, Maria Schneider examines the sad state of male reading habits: "Karen Holt, deputy editor of *Publishers Weekly,* says: 'The gap starts early, as girls in elementary and middle school read a lot more than boys, picking up a lifelong habit that most men never develop. Whether by cause or effect, most novels are published with women in mind.'"

As a public speaker, I travel the country frequently. I live out of a suitcase so much, I sometimes forget what closets are for. Everywhere I go, I talk about reading books. And without fail, I'm approached by people afterward—usually men, often executives, athletes, or busy professionals—who are convicted about their personal reading habits.

Somehow, instinctively, *we know we need to read.* Why is that so? What is it in this message that resonates? Is it just because our mothers told us so? I'm grateful I had a mother who modeled reading for me as a child, but I believe it's more than that.

Do you know that people were reading as far back as 6,000 years ago? In ancient Egypt, before there was a recorded alphabet, people would draw pictograms, which evolved into hieroglyphics. The pictures represented what we know today as verbs and phonetics. Our earliest books were often things like clay tablets and scrolls.

Now I don't know about you, but it's all I can do to write down everything I'm thinking about fast enough on my favorite note-taking device—the back of an envelope—even using a nice, sharp

No. 2 pencil. Those early authors have my admiration for their dedication to record their thoughts. It's clear the need to communicate through writing and reading has been around since mankind began to multiply on this Earth.

Have you ever rightly considered what the mere ability to read means? That it is the key which admits us to the whole world of thought and fancy and imagination? To the company of saint and sage, of the wisest and the wittiest at their wisest and wittiest moment? That it enables us to see with the keenest eyes, hear with the finest ears, and listen to the sweetest voices of all time?

—James Russell Lowell, nineteenth-century poet, editor, and writer

---

Reading puts us in direct contact with ideas from others. If you've ever sat in on a brainstorming session, you've experienced that electricity, that spark that leaps through a room when great minds come in contact. Imagine sitting in a room with a good book and having a brainstorming session—seemingly all by yourself! I've done it. People think you've lost it. Oh, if they only knew! Books do that. And books do so much more.

Reading Is Radical

So what about the future of books? In an interview on public television's *Between the Lines,* host Barry Kibrick asked author Lynne Truss (*Eats, Shoots & Leaves*) if she thought books as we know them, with covers and pages, would eventually morph into e-books to be read from screens. I confess I was a little disheartened to hear her agree that this would likely happen in time. Well, it's a good thing we read, as long as we read something—but give me an old-fashioned book I can hold in my hands anytime. Adobe e-publishing general manager Bill McCoy made my heart sing when he told *Forbes* magazine: "When we look out ten years from now . . . a lot more reading will be digital, but bookstores won't have gone away" ("Stop Worrying About Copyrights," Jonathan Enfield, *Forbes* magazine, December 11, 2006).

One thing is clear—books, no matter what technology comes up with in the future, have revolutionized our world. From the day Johannes Gutenberg rolled his first Bible off his brand-new printing press on August 24, 1455, life changed. Books opened new worlds to people who'd never known reading before. Gutenberg's Bible was so revolutionary, in fact, that it threatened the established church. For centuries, church leaders had controlled what the masses believed. Finally, people could read God's Word for themselves. Imagine it!

I fear the day when the technos decide that paper books are obsolete and we are reading from PC screens and iPods and eBooks, and we never again experience the little rush of opening a new book and cracking the spine and smelling the print and diving deep into the thoughts of the writer.

—Suzanne Somers, "Books Are," *Forbes* magazine, December 1, 2006

Novelist Victor Hugo paid homage to Gutenberg's invention when he wrote in his classic novel, *The Hunchback of Notre Dame,* "Human thought discovers a mode of perpetuating itself . . . Gutenberg's letters of lead . . . supersede Orpheus's letters of stone . . . The invention of printing is the greatest event in history."

A similar paradigm shift occurred in America when Ben

Franklin and a group of philosophical cronies known as the Junto created the Library Company of Philadelphia and the first public lending libraries in 1731. For years, books had been the exclusive domain of the aristocratic class, far too costly for the average person to obtain. But when these men pooled their resources to create something from which they could all benefit, they revolutionized society and opened the doorway for millions of imaginations to soar. We owe a great debt of gratitude to Ben for many reasons ... not the least of which is for making books accessible.

The real purpose of books is to trap the mind
into doing its own thinking.

—Christopher Morley,
early twentieth-century writer and editor

Books have the potential to shape your thinking as nothing else can. They influence both your attitude and your choice of other activities.

Andrew Solomon, author of *The Noonday Demon: An Atlas of Depression*, responded to the NEA findings in a *New York Times* op-ed, dated July 10, 2004. "[The study] also indicates that people who read for pleasure are many times more likely than those who don't to visit museums and attend musical performances, almost three times as likely to perform volunteer and charity work, and almost twice as likely to attend sporting events. Readers, in other words, are active, while nonreaders— more than half the population—have settled into apathy. There is a basic social divide between those for whom life is an accrual of fresh experience and knowledge, and those for whom maturity is a process of mental atrophy. The shift toward the latter category is frightening ... That the rates of depression should be going up as the rates of reading are going down is no happenstance."

Solomon then points to the dark era during World War II when Nazi leaders Adolf Hitler and Joseph Goebbels had books from the university burned in the plaza. They feared that ideas spurred by books could undermine armies. During the bleak years of Soviet domination, similar repression of literature occurred.

"The Nazis were right in believing that one of the most powerful weapons in a war of ideas is books," Solomon went on. "And for better or worse, the United States is now in such a war. Without books, we cannot succeed in our current struggle against absolutism and terrorism."

The Washington press corps
knows how to handle ambition; they
don't know what to do with ideas.

—Newt Gingrich, author,
Winning the Future: A 21st Century Contract with America

Virtual life may be trendy, but trends pass quickly. Trust me on this—I've seen more than a few of them come and go. For a while, my wife, Ruth, and I had sixteen teenagers in the family all at one time. In our house, trends were beginning and ending faster than point scoring during an NBA basketball game. Books offer ideas, thoughts, and knowledge that can spark action with a power to overcome even the most despicable evil. We need those ideas now more than ever.

The *Fear* Factor:
So What Can I Do About It?

I'm so glad you asked. If winning this war against the decline of reading is to be achieved, each of us must play our part. Here are a few solid suggestions. In fact, we've included a list like this at the back of every factor section to help you make your own decisions.

1. **Be aware of how you spend your time.** Is reading on your daily schedule? What books are you reading right now, in addition to this one? I find having more than one book going at a time challenges my brain more. What's next on your list? Plan to read, just as you calendar other events in your life. When you determine to make books a regular part of your life, every day, you'll be surprised at the personal growth you'll observe in just a few months.

2. **Remember that tomorrow is up to us.** It takes a concerted effort to keep what matters from becoming lost over time. We can think an activity is a good idea, but unless we recognize its importance, it most likely won't happen. That's true of anything worth doing. Reading matters. I cannot think of anything more tragic, more heartbreaking, than a world where no one reads. Do ideas matter to you? How else will they live on to reach, teach, and touch other lives if they are not written in a book? Books, by the way, are one of the greatest idea-processing machines ever invented. Not only did the author take time to think through what he or she wrote, but as your mind engages with that author's thoughts, you'll get all new thoughts—all your own. Make sure you keep a notebook handy. You never know when genius might strike! I've learned the hard way that an idea not recorded is often a brainchild never born.

3. **Determine to be part of the solution where reading is concerned.** When other people in your life see that reading matters to you, they'll be inspired to follow your lead. An *Orlando Sentinel* survey in December 2005 noted that of the top five leisure-time activities among Orlando citizens, reading did not even make the grade. Yes, Orlando has a lot of choices for spending time that other, more rural parts of the country may lack, but this is a huge indicator, in my mind, of where we are headed when too many choices crowd out reading. This is one place where you, my reading friend, can make a huge difference. Let people know that reading matters to you.

4. **Keep yourself abreast of the facts.** Read those NEA reports when they're released and make sure you're always involved in improving education in America, even if it's just writing letters to the editor about your local school board.

    Columnist and national observer David Gergen recently wrote, "Already, more than twice as many engineers, computer scientists, and information technologists are graduating in China as in the United States. All of this suggests that to maintain its edge, America no longer needs evolution in its schools—we need revolution" ("The Danger of Drift," David Gergen, *U.S. News and World Report,* May 29, 2006). Folks, future generations depend on us!

5. **Make sure you're aware of trends, both good and bad.** Don't be guilty of walking through life with blinders on. Books help you look in all directions—behind you, left to right, and straight ahead. Through books, you can study the past, see what's going on around you, and sometimes forecast tomorrow.

    Warning signs are just that—they warn us of impending danger. If we heed them, our chances of surviving the danger are good. But if we ignore them, we put at risk ourselves and our posterity. Reading is in trouble—do you admit that? Let's look at what these danger signs mean, and how we can avoid the falling rocks and sharp curves ahead.

Read for
Your Life
Way No. 2:

Combat the
Reality Factor

2

The Battle for
Hearts and Minds

"Pat," I hear you saying, "I get it. We don't read enough. Okay, you're right. But it's not like you to be so negative. Isn't there any *good* news you can share?"

Of course there is, my friend. In fact, in many ways, the future has never looked brighter.

Nearly one year after the NEA report cited in Chapter 1 was published, *Publishers Weekly* senior director Andrew Grabois spoke optimistically about the dramatic growth of the publishing industry during the twentieth century—a growth pattern that continues into the twenty-first. The industry, Grabois wrote, "has come a long way since the so-called Golden Age of the 1920s, when *Publishers Weekly* estimated that there were only 5 million people that ever bought a book that wasn't a Bible—or even twenty years ago, when any single Fortune 500 company generated more revenue than the entire book industry."

Grabois went on to speak of the more than 190,000 books published in 2004 alone as an indicator that "there appears to be more than enough power for this joy ride to continue." He's right. The publishing industry has become big business in the last couple of decades, and that's a good sign.

But the question remains—will the numbers of readers be able to keep up with the numbers of books? An article by Susan Driscoll and Diane Gedymin released in late 2006 reported a 10 percent decline in new titles in 2005. Michael Blake, author of *Dances with Wolves,* recently commented, "Nobody reads anymore . . . I read a reputable survey that said Americans read 24 million fewer books (over a year). That is a terrible symptom of a country in decline." I agree.

If people prefer to give away their limited time on this Earth to pursuits that eat up their minutes—just waiting for the clock to run out—rather than enriching their lives through activities like reading, those books published each year will eventually become nothing but kindling for Ray Bradbury's fireman.

One problem might be that many Americans take the ability to read for granted. There are still many places in this world—even in our own country—where reading is a rare skill. Statistics tell us that roughly half the people in this world are functionally illiterate. That, my friends, is an alarming fact.

Illiteracy: A War We Have Yet to Win

As innovations in travel and communication have expanded our global reach tenfold over the past hundred years, many Americans might think illiteracy is a third-world problem—and in many ways, they are right. According to United Nations statistics published in 2000, "The present state of affairs indicates that almost 1.5 billion children and adults are either illiterate or on the way to becoming so in the near future. This trend is likely to continue as population explodes on a continuous basis." This is a global tragedy!

In 1993, the U.S. Department of Education released findings from the most detailed profile to date concerning literacy in America. Called the National Adult Literacy Survey (ALS), it evaluated adult skills in the areas of prose, document, and quantitative proficiency. What this report uncovered is the sad fact that almost 50 percent of adults in America were either functionally illiterate or had limited reading skills. Further, it cited reading scores among young adults as decidedly lower than the proficiencies for young adults who had participated in the 1985 National Assessment of Educational Progress.

In *Literacy for Life,* the 2006 Education for All (EFA) Global Monitoring Report, we are told that millions of adults are being stranded on the sidelines of society by policies that neglect literacy. This shortsightedness not only diminishes life, but it is impeding progress in both education and poverty reduction (The International Reading Association website, http://blog. reading.org/).

Orlando Sentinel columnist Mike Thomas wrote ("School-jumping Hasn't Made Better Readers," May 22, 2005) about some disquieting statistics in local schools. It turns out that the Florida Comprehensive Assessment Test (FCAT) scores, particularly among students from low-income families, revealed that only 4 percent of tenth-graders are reading at grade level. The rest have a lot of catching up to do. Worse, Thomas wrote, "[Eighty-three] percent of them flunked the FCAT reading test altogether. This puts them somewhere between illiterate and reading at an elementary grade level." The report goes on to specify that these scores followed significant improvements in school staffing and funding. Clearly, at least as I interpret it, this problem is not one likely to go away by throwing more money at it. Yes, the problem is primarily with low-income kids, but, as Thomas said, "the problem is less about the classroom than it is their unstructured lives."

*The economic leg doesn't do anything
if the kid can't read, has no skills for the job
market. If a kid doesn't know how to use a
computer and is not information-literate, there's
nothing the economy can do for that kid
except give him a minimum-wage job.
It's education. And, increasingly, it's education
to give these kids the skills they're going to need
for the twenty-first century, and the self-esteem
and the belief in themselves that they can
be part of the twenty-first century.*

—Colin Powell, "Staying Powell," *AARP The Magazine,* July & August 2006

By May 2006, headlines spelled out a discouraging story: "Grade 4 FCAT Results a Puzzle," said the front page of the Local and State section of the May 28, 2006, *Sentinel.* "Florida educators are at a loss to explain this year's peculiar fourth-grade reading scores, which dropped sharply statewide after rising steadily for the past five years."

I'm not trying to single out Florida here, but if things are this bad right here where I live, you and I both know the problem is far from isolated. The article did, by the way, go on to report that students in third, fifth, and sixth grades all posted better scores. Reports like this make my eyebrows rise in alarm. Trends are rarely entirely local. All indicators are, nationwide and across the board, that reading is in trouble.

In August 2006, an Associated Press article cited the biggest drop in SAT scores in thirty-one years. Among other dismal numbers, the College Board reported a five-point drop in reading scores among the nation's 2006 high-school graduates. Another report from the *Washington Post*, dated December 26, 2005, cites literacy rates among college graduates are declining. "Only thirty-one percent of college graduates can read a complex book and extrapolate from it," said Michael Gorman, president of the American Library Association. "That's not saying much for the remainder." No, it certainly isn't. Gorman, the article said, was shocked by how few freshmen entering college understand how to use a library or even enjoy reading for pleasure. Folks, we're talking about an American crisis!

African American columnist Bob Herbert, writing in the *New York Times* on December 26, 2005, reviewed a few lessons from history regarding the tragedy of slavery as played out in the pre–Emancipation Proclamation United States. But the focus of his piece was not the past. Rather, he aimed point-blank at the poor choices being made by so many in the black community today. "Another devastating aspect of slavery," Herbert wrote, "was the numbing ignorance that often resulted from the prohibition against the education of slaves. It was against the law in most instances for slaves to learn to read. Now, with education widely (though imperfectly) available, we have entire legions of black youngsters turning their backs on school, choosing instead to wallow in a self-imposed ignorance that in the long run is as destructive as a bullet to the brain."

Another wrinkle appeared when it was revealed recently that a large number of immigrants to America lack English reading skills—and are doing nothing to correct that situation. According to a recent study (National Assessment of Adult Literacy), 14 percent of our adult population has "below basic" reading skills—a number that has not changed since the early 1990s.

Columnist Manning Pynn warned of the link between illiteracy and poverty in an *Orlando Sentinel* column (May 21, 2006). Responding to reports of a decline in newspaper sales in Brazil (as well as throughout the United States), Pynn wrote that in this land where more than half of the people live in poverty,

"Choosing to buy a newspaper [said news ombudsman German Rey], is a decision to forego food . . . For many, no such decision is necessary: they can't read."

In addition to details regarding Latin America's crisis of poverty and crime, Pynn posed the question, "Are newspapers the solution to this tragedy?

"No, but a widespread ability to read and access information could go a long way toward that goal. Those very basic tools can help overcome the wealth disparity that leads, eventually, to such lawlessness."

Pynn went on to address the decline in Florida's FCAT tests and suggested that America has a lot to learn from São Paulo, Brazil. If we think their situation could not happen here, he suggested, we need to think again. "There are lessons for Americans—if only we will read the handwriting on the wall."

My concern is that if we don't address these issues soon, we may not even be able to read those walls—the ones that may soon be closing in on us.

We've looked pretty closely at the relationship between poverty and literacy in this brief discussion on literacy, but there are decidedly other factors involved in this battle. Writing for *USA Today* (August 17, 2006), Colorado commissioner of education William J. Moloney reaches beyond the poverty indicators to openly suggest the real reason American children suffer when it comes to reading scores is due to inadequately trained teachers. Moloney discloses that the problem addressed more than half a century ago in Rudolf Flesch's *Why Johnny Can't Read,* "has grown to epidemic proportions in which nearly one-third of all U.S. schoolchildren have serious literacy deficits." That poverty should be the only reason is blown out of the water by reports that tell us kids in poor Caribbean and African nations have "levels of English literacy that would be the envy of any U.S. city." Most alarming to me is Moloney's statement about the world we're marching into, one he sees as having "an increasingly complex information-based economy that will reward only those who have the skills to serve its changing needs." Work with me here, folks—we've got to do better than this! We owe it to our kids.

Even if we have the Internet and we have the world wired, if you cannot read or write, you're left out. There is just no hope for you in the twenty-first century.

—Rick Warren, author and pastor

Trends That Spell T-R-O-U-B-L-E

And then there is the text messaging so popular with teenagers today. While educators are divided on its potential effect on reading and grammar, I say—look out! A column in a recent technology newsletter reported that "teachers say they're seeing the messaging lexicon show up in kids' schoolwork. Does Shakespeare lose something in translation to '2 b R not 2 b'?

"Some experts say the problem is not the lingo itself, but the fact that kids are unable to differentiate between when it is and isn't appropriate. Like slang and other informal language, what's okay for chatting with peers is not acceptable when writing an essay—or applying for a job" (Deb Shinder, *WXPnews,* January 17, 2006). If this picture is already being seen in our classrooms, it won't be long before it seeps into our culture as a whole. We need to be aware!

Kids need borders. They need guidance and parameters set on their activities. That need doesn't go away just because they've entered puberty. In fact, it becomes greater during those critical teen years. Parents and teachers—listen! This is *not* a hopeless situation. Instead, it's an opportunity to turn the lives of these young people around. Catching them in the elementary years is best, but I believe reading can be taught at any age, to anyone who wants to learn. I can't say it enough—having a teachable spirit that longs to learn is critical to survival in a world that is only going to become more competitive.

Reading lifts people up. It inspires us and challenges us to become better than we are today. Conversely, not reading keeps us suppressed and wallowing in failure. Among inmates in California prisons alone, the illiteracy rate is said to be greater than 80 percent! Just think how many lives might have been spared, how many who've gotten off on the wrong foot might have been turned toward a positive course if they had only been taught how to read.

Do these facts concern you? They should. No one should have to live with illiteracy. It's a problem we can and must solve! But it's about more than just the inability to read—it's about recognizing the importance of reading.

If people do not value reading, if we fail to master and pass on valuable reading skills, we may very well be doomed as a culture. Don't get me wrong here—people who know me know I'm an eternal optimist—but even I can admit it when the box scores mean the team is having a bad year.

Reading, after all, is one way we stay alive. Through books we pass ourselves on to the next generation. We'll talk more about that later on, but for now I urge you to recognize this fact: if future generations can't read, none of our lives will have much lasting difference. Is that the legacy you want to leave? I know it's not my choice.

America is a world leader. Billions of people around the globe follow our example. Rick Warren, author of *The Purpose-Driven Life* and pastor of Saddleback Church in Lake Forest, California, recently unfolded a huge plan to reach the world. He calls it the PEACE Plan—and it's one that might just work. Warren has identified what he believes are the five giants currently causing most of the world's problems and has developed a master strategy for taking them down. One phase of the plan involves educating people in other countries. As Americans, we need to lead the world out of illiteracy. But how are we going to do that if we don't lead ourselves out first?

Life Interrupted

Renowned social thinker and author Norman Mailer, writing for *PARADE* magazine in January 2005, asserted that American commercial television with its profit-driven pattern of interrupting programs every ten to fifteen minutes is a major culprit in killing our ability to concentrate. Pointing to the drop in percentage among young readers revealed in the NEA report, Mailer added: "High-school students were showing reduced interest in books . . . If the desire to read diminishes, so does one's ability to read. The search for a culprit does not have to go far. There are confirming studies all over academia and the media that too many hours are devoted each day to the tube. Television is seen as the culprit, since the ability to read well is directly related to one's ability to learn. If it is universally understood that the power to concentrate while reading is the royal road to knowledge, what may not be perceived as clearly is how much concentration itself is a species of psychic strength. It can be developed or it can go soft in much the manner that body muscle can be built up or allowed to go slack . . . Sixty years ago, children would read for hours. Their powers of concentration developed as naturally as breathing."

Mailer argues that children who throw tantrums when their play is interrupted are natural evidence for the fact that commercials interrupt the flow of concentration. In addition, they send the signal to children that concentration is "not one's friend but is treacherous."

Too much TV-watching can harm children's ability to learn and even reduce their chances of getting a college degree, three new studies suggest in the latest effort to examine the effects of television on children.

—Lindsey Tanner, "Too Much TV May Hurt Kids' Learning,"
Associated Press, July 2005

Former President Richard M. Nixon, himself a highly educated man, may have agreed with Mailer had they compared notes. "I would say I am concerned the most about the enormous power of television," Nixon once said. "I think the younger generation will come out less well-educated than would be the case if they could read more . . .

"There are so many good books out there . . . so many good articles that are thoughtful to read. It is something people have lost if they sit in front of the tube and turn off their minds . . . My best advice to any young person moving up is: read more, look at television less."

Reading Opens Doors to Your Future

What do you want to do with your life? Where do you want to go? No matter what stage of life you're currently in, if you're still breathing, you have a future. Whatever your goal, you need to know that someone has been there before you. Someone has probably written a book or books about exactly what you have in mind. Maybe you're already following a life plan and are involved in your chosen profession. In that case, books can help you do what you do even better. Wherever you are, someone has been down the same path you are on. Someone has a different perspective on what you're doing. Someone who's written a book can help you see what you're doing a little differently. Why not accept the challenge to accomplish more, keep your outlook fresh, and look at life from all sides? Books can help you do all those things.

In one of his Breakfast with Fred moments, leadership mentor and author Fred Smith relates: "In a book I read recently the author says that some people get up to age thirty-five or forty, level off and never climb any higher. He said that during the younger part of your life just being alive is enough to drive you forward, but then that energy starts to level off and unless you have a spiritual urge to drive you forward, the physical urge runs out and you level off. The non-physical urge that drives you forward is the thing that is a great motivation.

"One of the great sources of motivation is reading. We can't keep up without reading . . . Do you say, 'What do I need to read to improve me?' Until you do, you miss the best of reading."

Here are some facts I read recently that I don't like: according to the U.S. Census Bureau, the adults around you are likely to spend seventeen times as many hours watching the tube as they do reading books.

—Bill O'Reilly, *The O'Reilly Factor for Kids*

Do you know there is almost no topic that has not been written about in a book somewhere? If more people could read—if more people *would* read—it's just possible many of the world's problems could be drastically reduced, perhaps even eliminated altogether. So much of what is wrong today—from world hunger to AIDS—is still with us simply because of ignorance. When we educate people, when we teach them to read, they can learn to help themselves. Think about that for a few moments. There is a lot of power in knowing how to read.

Now, what about you? Do you know how to read? If you do, thank God and the person, or persons, who taught you! In my home as I was growing up, my mother set the example. We had books everywhere, and reading was a required part of our day. It wasn't work—it was fun. She created an atmosphere that generated excitement for reading in each one of us kids. *Thank you, Mom.* I can't say it enough, and doubtless you'll find my words of gratitude a few more times in these pages.

Who do you need to thank?

If you struggle with reading, if reading is a trial for you, there are places where you can find help. Look in your community services directory. Check the yellow pages for reading tutors. Talk to someone at your local library. But whatever you do, *do something!* Knowing how to read is critical to your survival in this world. Not knowing how to read is less a thing to be ashamed of than it is a problem to be faced and solved. Fear is conquered by moving against it, not by collapsing at its feet.

In Florida, my home state since 1986, high-school educators have been realizing an increase in students who lack basic reading skills. According to a January 2005 report in the *Orlando Sentinel,* Seminole County officials had just (at the time of the report) launched a three-year research project to determine where and why so many kids are falling through the cracks.

One indicator that a crisis was looming was the poor FCAT reading scores cited a few pages ago. "In order for kids to succeed in all of their classes," said Seminole High School principal Walt Griffin, "they have to have reading skills." Let me add to Principal Griffin's words: it's been my experience in every corner of life that in order for kids to succeed, period, they need reading skills.

The fact that you are reading this book right now indicates you understand that books matter. In your heart, you know you need to make reading a life priority. Maybe you have a longing to teach reading to others; perhaps you're a business leader who needs to read to keep up with trends in your world, or who wants to motivate others to greater achievement in their lives—whether it's your employees, your peers, or your kids. Perhaps you've been a reading teacher for years, and now you sense a stirring to take that gift out to the world. We'll talk about what you, personally and specifically, can do to help solve this reading dilemma later on in this book. For now, know that if you can read, you're one of the privileged few. You have a skill that is rare and precious. Cherish it—by using it!

Those who understand the code represented by the twenty-six letters of our alphabet have the key to unlocking untold treasures. The power of the written word is awesome: it inspires, it instructs, it takes us places we might never go on our own. Books introduce us to people and ideas. For many people, it was a book that set the course of their lives.

Here's another reason why failure to read is a problem, and this one is huge. In a *USA Today* interview with Bob Minzesheimer regarding his book *1776*, author David McCullough points out this startling fact: in our post 9/11 American society, McCullough said, "we're up against an enemy who believes in an enforced ignorance."

Whether or not you ever join the military, and no matter what your opinion is regarding war, you must realize the danger knell this statement rings. If we fail to reinforce our national intelligence through strong, free, and educated individuals, the enemy won't have to enforce ignorance. We'll have done it to ourselves.

---

*A wise person is hungry for knowledge,
while the fool feeds on trash.*

—Proverbs 15:14 (NLT)

Historically, book burnings were always carried out by despotic governments or power bases terrified by what would happen if people learned to think for themselves. Remember our discussion of the Gutenberg Bible just a few pages ago? Those in power were afraid that if the people could read the Bible for themselves, they would know that much of what they were being taught was in error. Truth sets us free. That's why petty, power-hungry tyrants fear books. Books have that much power!

In that *USA Today* article, David McCullough went on to say of those who fought the American Revolution, "Those people discovered the power of thinking for yourself. They had a love of learning." The question you must ask yourself is this: "Do *I* understand this power?" If you do, don't put off reading another day. Make a plan to be a lifetime reader now!

Not long ago these words in a devotional by writer John Fischer grabbed my attention: "Anorexia and bulimia are mind-crippling diseases that only function where food is plentiful. There are way too many starving people on this Earth, but most of them can't help it. Where they live there is not enough food to go around. It is ironically tragic that people can starve to death in the midst of plenty.

"What happens in the physical world is almost always an illustration of something like it in spiritual realms. And in spiritual terms, there is nothing more tragic than to have Christians starving spiritually with an overabundance of Bibles and teachers everywhere."

He is so right. And may I add it is equally tragic to have starving minds in a nation brimming with bookstores and books, simply because we'd rather do something else. Don't let this story be yours. Make a difference: read a book today and nourish your mind!

3

It's Up to You!

The American Booksellers Association's findings from a recent survey concluded that the average person reads fewer than two books per year. And of those, 97 percent think that reading the first two chapters of that book is enough. Well, who wants to be average? I once read that "the average salesman doesn't read a book a year. That is why he is the average salesman." I've been in the professional sports world for forty-five years, and I can tell you that average athletes have short careers.

At one point in Bradbury's *Fahrenheit 451*, fireman Montag meets a man named Faber, a reclusive former literature professor. "The public stopped reading of its own accord," Faber told Montag. "So few want to be rebels anymore."

Rebellion is *not* something I, Pat Williams, father of nineteen children, would normally encourage. But when it comes to reading, I urge you, for your benefit and that of your posterity, *to rebel against the trends of today!*

Read, read, read.

Books Are Healthy Choices!

Books are health food for your brain and dessert for your soul. Books are one of the few proven sources of mental exercise known to man. Reading is a workout for your mind. If your body needs thirty minutes of exercise a day, so does your thinker.

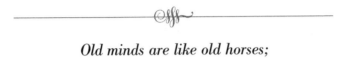

Old minds are like old horses;
you must exercise them if you wish to
keep them in working order.

—John Adams, second president of the United States

One scene in *Fahrenheit 451* finds a frustrated Montag arguing with his wife, Mildred, a woman who accepts her wall-to-wall television and no-books way of life without question.

> "Let me alone," said Mildred. "I didn't do anything."
> "Let you alone! That's all very well, but how can I leave myself alone? We need not to be let alone. We need to be really bothered once in a while. How long is it since you were really bothered?"

Let me put that same question to you, my friend. How long has it been since you were really bothered about the issue of reading books? As Bradbury's protagonist Montag suggests, we need not to be let alone. In the next chapter, we'll unpack a few facts about why reading—and reading books, in particular—is crucial to our success and survival. But first, let's talk a little more about the life-time benefits of books.

Books Are a Source of
Continuing Education

Earlier I directed my remarks toward American men, but the truth is that it doesn't matter who you are, where you are, what you do, or how old you are. Burton Rascoe, mid-twentieth-century critic and literary editor for the now-defunct *New York Tribune*, once observed, "The best-educated men and women I have known have been self-educated. This is true even of those who have been to college, for they did not go to college with an attitude, so often prevailing among students, of 'I dare you to educate me!' but with an eagerness to learn, an eagerness that sent them to good books."

Whether you are nine or ninety, college-educated, home-schooled, public-schooled, or unschooled, there are *books* for you to read and grow better by.

Here are some facts you need to know:

- The modern era is generally considered to have started in AD 1500 with the use of the printing press. From AD 1500 to 1830, all known knowledge doubled. From 1830 to 1930 all known knowledge doubled again. A few years ago, all known knowledge was doubling every fifteen to seventeen months. Today, all known knowledge is doubling *every sixty-three days,* and over the next three to five years, all known knowledge will double *every day*.

- There are more e-mail addresses in the world today than there are "snail mail" destinations. And only a few years ago, who had ever heard of e-mail?

- There are more websites in the world than there are families, and there are over a billion families in the world.

- If you took all the material floating around on the Internet in any given month, put that information into books averaging 250 pages, then stacked the books straight up, they would go over 200 million miles beyond the sun. And keep in mind, the sun is 93 million miles from Earth.

The world, it is a-changing. If you are not on the cutting edge of learning every day, you will be flushed out of the parade of life so quickly that all you will be able to do is stand on the sidewalk and wave as it passes you by. And if you are struggling with change, think how it will feel to be irrelevant.

The *Reality* Factor:
So What Can I Do About It?

How do you prevent this from happening? Very simple: make a commitment—*today*—to become a lifelong learner. Then go out and encourage others to do the same. We are in this world for such a short period of time. If you're young right now, this may sound like a tired expression, but trust me, one day soon you'll be repeating it to your children and grandchildren. My friend, don't let your page in the history books be one that's never read— simply because you failed to pass on this vital skill.

How do you become a lifelong learner?

1. **Continue your formal education.** Perhaps you never finished high school. Go get your GED. Maybe you never finished college or pursued your master's degree or went for your Ph.D. Now's the time to do it. Through distance learning and the power of the Internet, you can get it done without taking up residence on a college campus.

   When the last of our children left home in 2005, my wife Ruth decided to go back to school. Earlier in life, she'd gotten her undergraduate degree at LSU and a master's degree at Rollins College, but she'd always wanted her doctorate. So even though she's working full-time for FranklinCovey, she is now attending Walden University to work on her Ph.D. in organizational leadership. She's not on a campus, but takes advantage of their distance-learning program. It will take about three years, but by the time Ruth hits her sixtieth birthday, she will have her doctorate—and I will be married, at that point, to Dr. Ruth!

There are more options today for continuing your education than ever before. Like my Ruth, you can use one of the many online or by-mail mentoring programs offered by so many quality institutions. Whatever you do, please realize there is really no excuse to miss out on all life has for you because you lack a formal education.

2. **Remember, your brain is a muscle, like any other muscle in the human body.** It needs to be vigorously exercised on a regular basis so it won't become a pitiful mass of flab in an incredibly brief period of time. An unexercised arm or leg muscle will atrophy, and the same goes for your brain.

Nautilus and Hammer Strength have invented equipment to attach to every muscle of the human body—except your brain. They're working on it! But until they perfect it, I recommend a wonderful device that attaches perfectly to the brain and gives it an intense aerobic workout every time you make the attachment. The device is called a book, and the exercise is called reading.

Despite the proliferation of mega-bookstores and neighborhood reading groups, most Americans are indifferent to the lure of literature: in fact, according to a Wall Street Journal article of a few years ago, some 59 percent of Americans don't own a single book. Not a cookbook or even the Bible.

—Maureen Corrigan, writer and literature professor

3. **Challenge yourself to grow.** Not long ago, I spoke to a group of young people at Student Leadership University (SLU). One of them, young Brandon Dillow, contacted me later to let me know how much the conference meant to him. During SLU, this ninth-grade student challenged himself to read six hundred books before he begins college. That's almost two hundred books a year!

Friends, I urge you to make the world in which you live, the time in which you live, historic for absorbing knowledge, using knowledge, and passing it on. No matter what kinds of electronic marvels we invent, books have long been and continue to be the best place for that kind of information exchange to take place.

Later in this book, I'll outline my personal reading challenge. I present this challenge wherever I go in my travels—it's the same call to action that spurred young Brandon into reading readiness. Simply put, I challenge you to read for one hour a day from a book. It will change your life. Don't miss it; don't skip it; don't overlook it.

I'm making this as easy on you as I possibly can because I want you to do this! And I know you can. This book is a great place to start! Be like Brandon Dillow.

You may never again meet someone who cares so much about whether or not you read. But I do. So listen to Uncle Pat. Make reading a daily habit; encourage others to read. The secret is that you have to want to do it, too. I guarantee this: once you discover how tremendous books are, you'll be glad you became a reader.

Author Mark Eppler cites the reading activities of one contemporary creative-thinking expert: "Mike Vance recommends three hundred books a year. The fact that his suggestion is greeted with derision is a reflection not on Vance, but on our poor reading capabilities" (*The Heart of the Matter*, AMACOM/American Management Association, 2003, page 129). Three hundred a year, almost one a day, may seem a little extreme for most of us—but all of us should set some kind of reading goal. How many books a year? A month? A week? Write down a number and challenge yourself to meet it.

Maybe you haven't spent much time up to now thinking about reading and why it matters. In the next few chapters of this book, we're going to examine the mechanics of reading—the why, what, when, where, who, and how elements. Then we'll offer some practical steps you can take toward living a reading lifestyle. We're going to answer questions you may have, like:

- Why do books matter?
- When can I fit books into my already crowded schedule?
- What kinds of books should I read?
- Where are the best places to read?
- Who really cares about books?
- How can I conquer my bookstore phobia?
- How can I improve my reading habits and make reading a meaningful, interactive part of my everyday life?
- I already know reading matters, but what can I do to convince those I care about that they need to read, too?

One more thing before we get started: make sure you have your "fast passes" handy—you know, those things also known as your library cards, reading glasses, bookmarks, highlighters— whatever tools you need to take along. The adventure is about to begin.

Read for Your Life Way No. 3:

Remember the *Why* Factor

4

Read to Feed Your Mind

I have some news for you that may be hard to hear, so brace yourselves: *You don't know everything.*

Trust me on this.

As much as I read, it would be fair to say I'm a man who *wants* to know everything—but I can't. No one can. Knowing everything is impossible! Last I heard, only God could do it.

The things you're looking for, Montag, are in the world, but the only way the average chap will see 99 percent of them is in a book.

—Professor Faber in *Fahrenheit 451*

Now here's the *good* news: while it's true that none of us can know everything, we can all know more tomorrow than we do today.

The question is—do you *want* to know more? I know I do. If you do, too, then answer this somewhat rhetorical question: how can you and I learn if we don't read? You won't get smarter from video games, chat rooms, or from spending more time in the office.

Faber, Ray Bradbury's fictitious professor, understood that knowledge is a treasure to be pursued, and that most of it is found in books. You need to get that picture, too. Video games come and go; movies, while there are many great ones, are often forgotten as soon as the Oscar ceremony has ended; TV shows last maybe an hour or two. And who can keep up with the iPod? Don't get me wrong—I'm not knocking any of these forms of entertainment. But I am urging you to understand that books are deserving of at least as much time as these other pursuits—and, I'd argue, *far more*!

When we read, our imaginations are stimulated by the natural desire to *see* the characters or the setting being described. Ideas are born when we read—ideas for how to start businesses, motivate leaders, spark winning basketball teams—or even write more books. Television, movies, and other forms of electronic entertainment have their place, to be sure, but if you want a lively, productive imagination, there's no substitute for what you can find between the covers of books. Our minds are capable of pictures that cameras can only *want* to see.

Language is the soul of intellect, and reading is the essential process by which that intellect is cultivated beyond the commonplace experiences of everyday life . . . Reading is a means of thinking with another person's mind; it forces you to stretch your own.

—Charles Scribner, Jr., publisher

Art Linkletter told a story about someone visiting Disneyland during its fiftieth anniversary celebration in 2005. "Gee," the visitor said to Art, "it's a shame Walt can't be here to see this." Art responded, "He did see it. That's why it's here." If a man who grew up without television, video games, palm pilots, cell phones, or HDTV could create something as amazing as Disneyland, well, where do you think those ideas came from? Walt was a reader, my friends, with a great imagination. Because he loved stories, he wanted to share that love. So he made pictures to help you and me see them as he did. Let reading stimulate your imagination as it did young Walt Disney's.

Read to Change Your Life

As a child, Benjamin Carson spent his primary school years in the bottom of the academic pool. By the time he'd reached fifth grade, the nickname "Dummy" had become his permanent label. Then his mom took charge. Though she was a single parent who had been a teenager when Benjamin was born, she understood what needed to happen, and it didn't involve teachers' conferences. Ben's mom restricted his leisure time and insisted that homework and books come first. She insisted that Ben and his brother read two books a week, and to make sure they were retaining what they read, she asked for book reports, too. Young Benjamin hated it, but in eighteen months, he'd gone from the bottom of the class to the top.

One day, his science teacher asked the class a question about a rock sitting on the teacher's desk. Since he had just finished reading a book on geology, Benjamin knew the answer. No one else in class did. That was the moment Benjamin Carson understood what his mother was doing. Though unable to read herself, she knew her sons would not succeed in life without books. And today, Dr. Benjamin Carson is director of pediatric neurosurgery at the Johns Hopkins Hospital, and the first person to successfully separate Siamese twins connected at the head.

People don't realize how a man's whole life can be changed by one book.

—Malcolm X

In an interview for *Investor's Business Daily*, Dr. Carson told writer Curt Schleier, "You actually have to work when you read, just as you have to work when you lift weights. You have to take letters and make them into words so you learn how to spell. You have to take words and make them into sentences so you learn grammar and syntax. And you have to take these sentences and translate them into concepts. You don't have to do that when you're watching television. The concepts are already developed for you, so you don't become creative."

People who read are people who achieve. What are your life goals? It doesn't matter if you're ten or one hundred and ten; it's never too late to attain those goals. Books help you get there.

People who read are better communicators. Constant exposure to the written word can't help but impact and shape how we perceive and use language. It's well known that word power is a critical key to success. Do you want to increase your vocabulary? Books are full of words! What a great place to continue your education in language arts.

Mark Edmundson, author of *Why Read?* told C-SPAN interviewer Brian Lamb, "We all get socialized one time around by parents and teachers and schools and priests and ministers, and what have you. And for a lot of people, those values will do just fine. They're community values. They're long tested and long tried, and there's something eminently respectable about them.

"But there are other people who, for whatever reason, just don't fit right into the established values. They find themselves disgruntled, dissatisfied with what even the best-meaning teachers and parents said. Those people go a lot of directions, but one of the best directions they can go is to become obsessed readers. They read and read and read until they start to find people who see the world in a way that's akin to theirs. And then they feel that they're home. They've got a second set of parents and a second set of teachers, and they can start seeing the world for themselves, a little bit different from the way the community sees it, often."

Books inspire change. Dramatic, powerful periods in our lives are often triggered by a book—or books—we've read. Can you think of a book that changed your life? It's a question worth asking yourself. What books have made a difference for you? If your answer is "none," may I suggest you find one?

When I was just seven years old, I was dynamically influenced by one of the first books I ever read. My dad gave me a copy of *Pop Warner's Book for Boys,* and the course of my life was decided. Thanks in large part to that book, I have not only spent my entire professional life in the world of professional sports, but I've become a lifelong reader. In fact, I echo the words of the late poet Langston Hughes, who once wrote (*The Big Sea: An Autobiography,* Hill and Wang reissue, 1993), "Books began to happen to me." In addition, the lessons Pop Warner offered young athletes became foundational for me and continue to influence me—my concepts and beliefs regarding teamwork, sportsmanship, winning, leadership, and more—to this very day.

It may seem unusual to you that a man who's made his living in the world of sports would love books as much as I do. My friend Jerry B. Jenkins once called me a "Renaissance jock." I suppose that's a good description. It's how my parents raised me. Whatever you do for a living, that living can be enhanced—as mine has—by books.

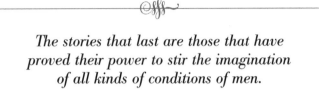

*The stories that last are those that have
proved their power to stir the imagination
of all kinds of conditions of men.*

−Walt Disney

Reading helps us understand life. It shouldn't be about just finding people whose opinions agree with yours, but about exposing your mind to new ideas, more information, and different perspectives. Reading, when done effectively, takes who we are and makes us more.

Here's another way in which reading changes our lives: research shows us that what we put into our minds puts us in charge of our lives. If we see negative images or read negative words, we become grouchy and ill at ease. Positive images—like those beautiful Rose Parade floats we see every January 1—bring sunshine into our hearts and minds, even if we live in subzero climates when we see them.

Oh, I know there are those who argue there is no relationship between what we put into our minds and what we do, but please, you and I both know there is a decided connection. What you read, what you see, what you listen to truly influences your thoughts.

Earl Nightingale was a leading authority on success and on what makes people successful. Nightingale spoke of what he called a "strange secret": *You become what you think about.*

What we think about most definitely influences how we feel. While there is tremendous evidence today to support this idea, it is at least as old as the first century BC. The apostle Paul knew this and advised his Philippian readers, "Summing it all up, friends, I'd say you'll do best by filling your minds and meditating on things true, noble, reputable, authentic, compelling, gracious—the best, not the worst; the beautiful, not the ugly; things to praise, not things to curse" (Philippians 4:8, The Message).

Books give us so many choices, so many words, and so many ideas upon which to anchor and build what we think about. Choose wisely, my friends.

What goes into the mind comes out in a life.

—Motto of the Christian Booksellers Association

Read to Grow

When we open the cover of a book, we can't help but become a slightly different person by the time we've closed it. If we're careful to select books that challenge us rather than those that merely agree with us or tell us what we already know, we will inevitably grow in mental, intellectual, and spiritual stature. Let books challenge your potential.

"Words are enormously important to me," former New York Mayor Rudy Giuliani has said. "I love to read, and I love language . . . the sheer pleasure of words in the right order. Choosing one word over another is an important act."

Books help you grow in so many ways. I can think of at least four key ways in which reading contributes to your growth:

1. **Reading shapes your values.** As you read, especially books by and about people you admire, you'll learn how they think and feel—what's important to them. If your heart's desire is to emulate that person, you'll begin to adapt his or her values into your life. Chances are, they're close to those you already believe in. Reading helps you refine them. The great words and noble ideas you find in books help you clarify and define your values. As Rick Warren has written, "The way you see your life shapes your life."

2. **Reading shapes your thinking.** Great writers use powerful verbs and write in ways that can actually alter the way we think. What better example of that truth is there than in these words from the apostle Paul, who urged his readers, "Do not conform any longer to the pattern of this world, but be transformed by the renewing of your mind" (Romans 12:2, NIV)? *Reading actually transforms our minds.*

Books are compasses and telescopes
and sextants and charts which other men
have prepared to help us navigate the
dangerous seas of human life.

—Jesse Lee Bennett, twentieth-century American writer

---

3. **Reading helps determine your life course.** Our world is filled with stories of lives changed by books. Are you wondering what your life purpose is? Bookstores and libraries hold many of the answers you're seeking. Through books you might learn how to do some particular skill, or find inspiration to be like someone you admire.

Elsewhere in these pages I've mentioned a book my dad gave me when I was quite young—a book by the legendary Pop Warner. That book undoubtedly played a part in my later decision to invest my life in the world of professional sports. To be sure, growing up surrounded by baseball didn't hurt, either. But books helped my head know what to do with what my heart felt inside. The advice and experiences of others informed my dreams. Books can do that for you, too.

4. **Reading builds your character.** Who you are is largely determined at birth and is a combination of factors

inherited from your parents. This does not mean that the way we express our personalities will be carbon copies of those parents. My son Bobby and I, for example, share many of the same passions—we both love sports, we love reading, we believe in strong, exemplary leadership. But the way we manifest those beliefs is distinctly different.

Les Carpenter of the *Washington Post* wrote a great article about Bobby and me called "Father and Son Game" (July 7, 2005). In it, Carpenter pointed out that "Bobby Williams is as quiet as Pat is exuberant" and "Where Pat booms into a room like it's the Improv, throwing out one-liners, interrogating every new person he meets, talking in lists . . . his second-oldest child seems content to sit on the periphery, to watch and assess." Bobby and I share many qualities, but we are also our own distinct men.

The point is, you may have a veritable Williams household of characteristics inherited from your parents, and, yes, all those genetic qualities influence who you are. But with all that, you remain a uniquely created individual. You are you, and there will never be another one.

Books develop that uniqueness by exposing us to the ideas, experiences, and wisdom of those who've been down the paths we're on. They've seen the end from the beginning, and they can point out the twists, turns, and potholes up ahead of us. Books challenge us to be all we can be—and more. They are the road signs, the traffic police, the signals that help us stay on course.

It is not true that we have only one life to live; if we can read, we can live as many more lives and as many kinds of lives as we wish.

—S. I. Hayakawa, educator and politician

Other life influences and experiences, often not of our choosing, also impact who we become. Children, for instance, have little to no control over the home in which they are raised or who their parents are. For that reason, Mom and Dad, it's critical that we model great character traits for our kids.

Beyond those genetic factors, however, each one of us has the capacity to influence our character through the choices we make. Books are a primary factor in shaping our thoughts, attitudes, beliefs, and responses to situations. In other words, the characters we read about go a long way toward shaping our character. We'll talk more about the "who" factor in another chapter, but for now, know that the "who" in you is a great reason *why* you should read.

Read to Build Your Mind

Books build brains. It's true. Books are like weights and workout machines for our minds. What's more, we've known that for years. Is it possible that reading could be the answer to preventing such age-related tragedies as dementia and Alzheimer's disease? Writing in *U.S. News & World Report* (December 5, 2005), Dr. Bernadine Healy reported, "Alzheimer's is more apt to strike those who don't continually prod their intellects to learn and expand. Yes, use it or lose it. Brains are dynamic beings—growing nerve cells, establishing complex networks and connections, breaking down unneeded old ones. Exercising the brain builds reserves of neural networks." Dr. Healy advised, "The message to our children: study, study, study."

Not long ago, I picked up a copy of the book *Letters to Young Black Men* by Daniel Whyte III (Torch Legacy, 2005) and was thrilled to find his list of the seven benefits of reading:

1. Through regular reading you can become an "educated person" without following a rigid course of study.
2. Regular reading forces you to increase your vocabulary.

3. Through regular reading you can become a more interesting person to talk with.

4. Through regular reading, you are able to go places, mentally, that you may not be in a position to go physically.

5. Regular reading will help you become a better writer, speller, and speaker.

6. Regular reading helps you to become a thinker.

7. Regular reading puts you head and shoulders above the crowd.

Healy and Whyte understand what needs to happen to make us productive people in every way. No matter what age you are today, you can and should invest in your mental health, just as you would your physical health. Books are the best source of mind aerobics known to date.

Writer Holbrook Jackson once observed, "We read to train the mind, to fill the mind, to rest the mind, to recreate the mind, or to escape the mind." There are so many reasons to pick up a book, and every one of them involves your mind.

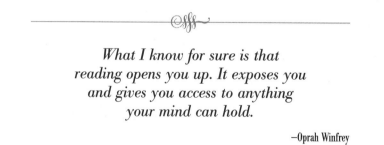

What I know for sure is that
reading opens you up. It exposes you
and gives you access to anything
your mind can hold.

—Oprah Winfrey

"Reading is to the mind what exercise is to the body," said eighteenth-century Irish writer Sir Richard Steele. Some things never change, and this truth is one of them. As pumping iron is great for our biceps, triceps, and deltoids, so pumping books through our brains strengthens our mental muscles.

Recently, I heard Rick Warren point out that training for the mind is the first step out of poverty. That thought alone should be enough to spur most of us to make reading a daily habit. For years, the slogan of the United Negro College Fund has been, "A mind is a terrible thing to waste." Books are one of the best mind- and time-wasting preventives I know. Fitness experts tell us that muscle burns fat, so build your mental muscle and put that brain fat to good use!

Read to Live Longer

Don't believe that reading can help you live longer? Many people believe that actively engaging your mind in books can extend your life. But in this case, what I'm talking about is living through the lives of others. Books can help you do that! I'm not getting metaphysical here. What I mean is that through books, we can meet new people and make contact with ideas and thoughts we wouldn't come up with on our own.

Learning through books extends our life goals, even when we're long past what the government calls "retirement age." That year arrived for me recently, but I have no plans to retire. I feel like I'm just getting started! Noted Bible teacher Chuck Smith, Sr., is known for his stated desire to "wear out rather than rust out." I agree! There is so much yet to learn from books. No single lifetime could hold it all.

"Reading sweeps the cobwebs away," wrote author Chuck Swindoll. "It enhances thinking. It stretches and strains our mental muscles. It clobbers our brittle, narrow, intolerant opinions with new ideas and strong facts. It stimulates growing up instead of growing old."

Read to Connect with Others

Communication is one of our first great needs in life. What is the first thing most babies do when they emerge from the dark womb in which they've spent their first nine months? They cry! And when they do that, they're communicating a message. Not yet having words at their disposal, they use what they do have—their lungs. In addition to being a natural tool for getting those lungs working, a newborn baby's cries tell those around him, "That light is too bright! And I'm hungry!"

Later, as that child grows and begins to use language skills, he discovers that words usually get him what he wants and are far more effective than whining noises.

Not long ago, I witnessed a familiar scene during a "discussion" between a young mother and her three-year-old daughter. The preschooler wanted something, but couldn't seem to get out what it was. In her frustration, her face turned red and screwed itself into a massive wet twist, reminiscent of one of our Florida hurricanes. She thrashed her arms and stamped her feet. Like a day trader watching the numbers for just the right moment, her mommy patiently waited for her opportunity. Sensing it, she went in for the kill. "Angie, calm down," she said, modeling her request. "I don't know what you want unless you use words to tell me." In time, Angie got the message. She may not have known all the words she needed yet, but she knew enough to get started.

One sure window into a
person's soul is his reading list.

—Mary B. W. Tabor, *New York Times* columnist

Language is empowering. Reading helps us learn more words. It helps us master our language. And with more words, our ability to communicate effectively with others only gets better.

Whether you lead a young family or a Fortune 500 corporation, you need to understand the power of communication in leadership. Leaders are people who see what needs to be changed and work to make it happen. They have a vision for how things can be better. Armed with that vision, a leader needs to know how to excite, inspire, and motivate everybody on the team into seeing his or her vision. If you can't do that, you'll lose every game you play, no matter how talented your players are. Books help you develop the message you need; they give you the words to communicate your vision. Read books in your field that help you learn better ways to get your job done, and then supercharge the doers with the new ideas those books inspire.

---

*In my contact with people I find that,
as a rule, it is only the little narrow people
who live for themselves, who never read good
books, who do not travel, who never open up
their souls in a way to permit them to
come into contact with other souls—
with the great outside world.*

—Booker T. Washington, *Up from Slavery*

There's another way that reading connects us with others, and it's one of the best reasons for reading of which I can think. When we read, we discover a huge, comforting truth: we are not alone.

No matter what problem you have that you think no one on Earth has ever experienced before, you're wrong. Someone else has not only been there and done that, but lived to tell about it in a book.

Author James Baldwin once wrote, "You think your pain and your heartbreak are unprecedented in the history of the world, but then you read. It was books that taught me that the things that tormented me most were the very things that connected me with all the people who were alive, or who had ever been alive."

Do you struggle with loneliness? Most of us do at some time or another. Yes, you could soak yourself in your tears, even be guest of honor at a fabulous pity party. But wouldn't you be better off to discover a way out of your misery? Wouldn't you rather invest your life in another person, do something for someone else's sake and not your own gratification? I'm convinced that books hold the answers to almost any problem—or excuse—we can imagine.

Read to Make Friends and Meet Influential People

Nineteenth-century writer Martin Tupper once wrote, "A good book is the best of friends, the same today and forever." Have you ever thought of a book as your friend? Most of us who love to read have held at least one or two books in high esteem. What's really going on is we're connecting with the mind of the writer.

What a writer writes is often different from what he or she might say in public—or even in private! There's something about putting our thoughts in writing that makes it easier to be transparent. So when we read, we are actually linking minds with that writer—sort of like secret friends, or "kindred spirits."

Let's face it: we have limited time on this Earth. Sooner or later, all of us lament over people with whom we didn't spend enough time, or those we never got to meet at all. Think of the millions who have gone on before us. Through books, those lost moments can be redeemed. Books enable us to touch the minds of people, both living and dead, we would otherwise never know. Through books, we who write achieve a level of immortality here on Earth.

A great book should leave you . . . slightly exhausted at the end. You live several lives while reading it.

—William Styron, author

Through books we reap the benefits of someone else's ideas and solutions. Things we may have puzzled about have already been through someone else's mental processor. Fortunately for the rest of us, some of those great thinkers have recorded their ideas in books.

My friend and frequent writing partner Jim Denney says in his book *Quit Your Day Job!* "I've always loved the feel of a book in my hands. The weight of a book is the substance of an author's thoughts pressing against your flesh." And, I might add, it's the spark of that author's words and ideas fusing with your thoughts. What greater way is there to connect with all humankind?

The *Why* Factor: So What Can I Do About It?

Make up your mind that reading matters. Whether or not it mattered to you up until this moment, it matters now. And it matters tomorrow. For your own sake, and that of everyone whose life you impact, make these decisions:

1. **Realize reading matters.** Entrepreneur and department store founder J.C. Penney regretted neglecting books in his youth. Fortunately, he lived long enough to make up for that mistake. "I should like to say to the young men in particular that it is a splendid thing to make money, but it is a greater thing to make a good way of life. If they will devote some

time each day to reading the best books they can find, they will derive a lasting benefit throughout their lives."

2. **Decide to work hard to discover great truth.** "To read books casually will not suffice," Penney continued. "One must study every sentence and make sure of its full message. Good writers do not intend that we should get their full meaning without effort. They expect us to dig just as one is compelled to dig for gold. Gold, you know, is not generally found in large openings, but in tiny veins. The ore must be subjected to a white heat in order to get the pure gold. So remember this when you read."

3. **Take hold of the power books have to change your life.** Oprah Winfrey, TV's daytime goddess of books, discovered this power during her extremely difficult childhood. "Books were my pass to personal freedom," she has said. "I learned to read at age three, and soon discovered there was a whole world to conquer that went beyond our farm in Mississippi."

4. **Read because you need to learn.** As I said at the beginning of this chapter, you don't know everything. Neither do I. But when we read, we learn things we didn't know before we read them. We gain a new perspective. Benjamin Disraeli, the late great prime minister of England, wisely observed, "To be conscious that you are ignorant of the facts is a great step to knowledge."

5. **Read because Mr. Rogers said so.** Now don't look at me like that—it's true! In his biography titled *I'm Proud of You: My Friendship with Fred Rogers* (Gotham, 2006), author Tim Madigan recalls, "I once asked him what he did for fun. He said, 'Read.' He did most of his reading at night, and usually in the field of spirituality and the human condition." Mr. Rogers taught generations of kids how to respect one another. Obviously, he remembered what he read.

Now that we all agree why reading matters, let's look at how to fit it into our already crowded daily lives.

Read for Your Life Way No. 4:

Resolve the *When* Factor

5

Finding Time

"Why should I read the book when I can just watch the movie?" It's the universal lament of nearly every student assigned to write a book report, and of way too many men who think they're "saving time" by watching the movie. Oh, but books and movies are such vastly different forms of communication.

Read the best books first,
or you may not have a chance
to read them at all.

—Henry David Thoreau

Movies may offer glorious visual images, but books let us crawl up inside the words. Movies tend to force-feed the story to us at the director's whim, whipping us from scene to scene so fast we barely have time to figure out what just happened before the credits start to roll (and roll and roll). Books let us linger.

They invite us to spend a little time with the characters we love, to thoroughly examine ideas, to wrestle with and fully grasp difficult concepts. With books, the story never has to end. We can open the book and go back again, anytime we want. Books call upon the power of our imagination in ways that movies often deny.

But who has time anymore? A United Press International article in September 2006 ("Survey Shows Many Have No Time for Books") cited a Chinese reading habits survey in which more than 40 percent of respondents said they have no time to read books. It's not just in America.

The fact is, we're all too busy. It's a stigma of our high-tech society. Never has so much been available for so many—information, ways to get information, potential to stay in touch with family, friends, and associates, opportunities to get the latest headlines as fast as the reporters can make them up. Thanks to Internet, e-mail, cell phones, and careers that long ago left a forty-hour workweek in the dust, "downtime" has become a relic for most of us. With all that stuff competing for our time and attention, what's a poor book to do?

Pat Schroeder, president of the Association of American Publishers, told *USA Today* (March 3, 2005) that people have been "convinced by the culture that they don't have enough time to read books."

Does that describe you? Do you think you don't have time to read? Here's what I've discovered: if something matters to you, you'll find a way to do it. Maybe reading needs to matter to you more. I hope by the end of this book, you're convinced to *make* time for books—for your sake and for the sake of those in your world.

After a long day at one of his various jobs,
he would read far into the night.
A steadfast purpose sustained him.

—Doris Kearns Goodwin on Abraham Lincoln

Horace Mann, the renowned early American educator, said, "Resolve to edge in a little reading every day, if it is but a single sentence. If you gain fifteen minutes a day, it will make itself felt at the end of the year."

Mann was right, but I believe he hedged on that advice. We need to see reading as critical to our health. I admit I don't have any hard facts to back this up, but my guess is if we all kept our minds active and engaged through daily reading habits, we would see a decline in the increase of diseases that affect the mind. We know, after all, that one cause of age-related mental diminishment is plaque buildup. We know how plaque builds up on our teeth, and we've developed tools for dealing with it. Isn't your brain as important as your teeth? So think of daily reading as mental dental floss!

Abraham Lincoln, America's sixteenth president, pursued reading with the passion of a starving man looking for food. Anytime was the right time to read, to Lincoln's way of thinking. Doris Kearns Goodwin writes of Lincoln: "Working simply to 'keep body and soul together' as a flatboatman, clerk, merchant, postmaster, and surveyor, he engaged in a systematic regimen of self-improvement. He mastered the principles of English grammar at night when the store was closed. He carried Shakespeare's plays and books of poetry when he walked along the streets. Seated in the local post office, he devoured newspapers."

Could Lincoln have been driven by a sense of urgency, knowing somehow his life would not be a long one? Whatever the reason, Abe Lincoln made the most of the time he was given. He spent much of it learning by reading.

Make Time!

I've said this before, but it can't be said enough: my personal favorite daily weight-lifting challenge is to pick up a book and read from it for at least one hour every day. Most days, I get in two to three hours. If I can do this with a full career, a crowded speaking calendar, and nineteen kids, I believe everyone can. Wherever I go on speaking engagements, I challenge my listeners to do what I do. With this book, I offer that same challenge to each of you.

Why not make that choice, too? Get up close and personal with words. Let them expand your mind and change your life.

Success trainer Brian Tracy offers these tips for squeezing more reading into your schedule: "Take advantage of every gift of time that you receive . . . Always carry reading material to go through when you get these unexpected moments of waiting or inactivity.

"If you read a book a month . . . you will read twelve books a year, one-hundred-twenty books in the next ten years, and you will become one of the best-read people in the world, by using this method. Or, if you read the classics for fifteen minutes a day, over the course of a few years, you would have read all the great books of literature."

We have advantages today that never existed before when it comes to reading. Many classic works are in the public domain and can be downloaded to your computer. You can print them out or read right from the screen if you choose. So you don't even need to buy books, necessarily, or even go to the library to check them out.

It's not that I don't like people.
It's just that when I'm in the company of others—
even my nearest and dearest—there always comes
a moment when I'd rather be reading a book.

—Maureen Corrigan, book critic for NPR's *Fresh Air*

Tools for Reading Anytime, Anywhere

In the last decade, computer search engines have revolution-ized our lives. As I am writing this book, I find the business head-lines literally bursting at the seams with news of what the folks at Google and Amazon are coming up with. Online book options are an ever-growing trend. Google Print provides a free service that allows authors and publishers to promote books, and offers readers a tool for finding books they'd miss otherwise. It's what you call a win-win situation, as their competitors are rapidly finding ways to innovate and offer more, too. Tools like these not only make research easier to do, but they make picking out your next book a much simpler task. You can "browse the stacks" right from home. For researchers, nothing is more promising. For readers, it's a decided option. To my mind, as long as it gets and keeps people reading, it's a great thing.

With all these electronic possibilities, however, I find I'm forced to agree with Dorothy Mays, research librarian at Rollins College in Winter Park, Florida. In comparing the book in the hand versus the text on the screen, Mays told the *Orlando Sentinel* (November 4, 2005), "A book is portable, lightweight, easier on the eyes."

Stephen Riggio, CEO of Barnes & Noble, agrees. He told *New York Times* columnist Ken Jaworowski (April 15, 2006), "[E-books and podcasts] are a very, very tiny market. As the writer Paul

Auster told me recently, the book is a perfect technology. If it were invented today, it would be revolutionary. It's user-friendly; it's portable. Books are relatively inexpensive. The have value as physical objects; they last a lifetime.

"Not all books can be converted into digital forms—just think about illustrated books and children's books."

Personally, I think books will always have a "hands-on" appeal. Were that not so, all brick and mortar bookstores would have gone the way of Amazon long ago. Libraries would be historical repositories and museums, rather than way stations for hungry minds. There's something decidedly more satisfying about holding a book in your hands rather than reading from a screen.

Ultimately, though, it doesn't matter whether you read a book in your hands, from the screen of your handheld computer, or listen to it on the way to work. However you do it, you receive the kinds of ideas you can only get from books.

I think one reason books have so much impact on our lives is because they require a little more time and several senses to process their information. When we converse with one another, we use our ears, our minds, and our mouths. When we listen, we use our ears and—hopefully—our brains as well. When we read an actual book, we use our hands, our eyes, our minds—and then sometimes our mouths to read a favorite part out loud to someone nearby. I even like the way books smell. Books urge us to take notes or write down the thoughts they stir up. Books are a literal interactive conversation and a complete sensory experience.

When people hear that I read, on average, five books a week, they are often amazed. But the truth is, I have the same number of minutes and hours in the day as you do. I've just been so motivated by my love for books that I've learned to use those "extra" minutes for reading: stoplights, doctor's offices, plane flights (I'll admit I may take more of those than the average person). And I've trained myself to read rapidly and retain what I've read. This is a valuable skill, which I believe anyone can learn at almost any age. We'll talk more about speed-reading later in this book. For now, let's apply some serious thinking to when we can make time to read.

---

*On my way to speaking engagements,
I'm always reading something I need to know
or preparing my next presentation. I'm a constant
student. I've read an average of more than three
hours a day for thirty-plus years, and I read a
wide range of materials—everything from
the Bible to several daily newspapers.*

—Zig Ziglar, motivational speaker and author

How Much Time Do I Need?

Business expert Jim Rohn advises us: "Hear or read something challenging, something instructional, at least thirty minutes every day. Miss a meal, but not your thirty minutes. You can get along without some meals, but you can't get along without some ideas, examples, and inspiration."

Old Sam Johnson took Rohn's advice—and even mine—a leap further when he recommended, "A young man should read five hours in a day, and so may acquire a great deal of knowledge."

I suppose we can all come up with something else to do these days, but my thanks go to the late great Groucho Marx, who observed, "I find television very educational. The minute somebody turns it on, I go to the library and read a good book."

If all you want is a pastime—if all you really want to do is sit there and be entertained until your time is up—then watch television. Even at its worst, TV passes the time. Maybe you can at least find a good NBA basketball game to watch.

But I believe you want to do far more than that with the time you've been given. If you didn't, you wouldn't be reading these words right now. Books will help you achieve your lofty goals, because through books you can take the collected wisdom of all those who've come before you—and build on it. Now isn't that idea worth turning off the tube, putting down the joystick, or saying "no thanks" to that party? I'm not saying we shouldn't do those things, too. Everything has its place, and some activities are meant for keeping in touch with others, building relationships, or just relaxing. I'm just encouraging you to consider your priorities—and give reading a higher place on the list. It really does deserve it.

If you think you're too busy to read, look at how other busy, successful people spend their time. My guess is you'll discover most, if not all, of them give reading some part of their day.

Washington Post writer Ann Gerhart reported on the reading habits of President and First Lady George W. and Laura Bush. "George and Laura start and end the day reading, with her often reading from the papers in the morning and both buried in books at night." Developing a habit like this may require setting the alarm clock a half hour earlier or propping up your bed pillows awhile before nodding off, but I believe you'll not only find that time well spent, you'll discover you don't miss the sleep you gave up.

Where do I find the time for not reading so many books?

—Karl Kraus, literary editor and publisher

Look for Empty Time to Fill with Books

If there is one thing that characterizes the times we live in, at least here in America, it is waiting. We wait at stoplights; we wait in lines at post offices, stores, movie theaters, and theme parks;

we wait in doctor's offices; we wait for job interviews. When we travel, which most of us do nearly every day to get to school or work, we even wait to get to our destination. "Hurry up and wait" is a theme song most of us have memorized.

My commute to work isn't a long one, but I've learned to make use of stoplights. Since I'm familiar with my route, I've studied those lights. I know their cycles, and I know just about how much time I've got when I'm waiting at one. I use that time to read.

Maybe you don't feel comfortable with the idea of reading at the wheel. I can understand that. I received a letter not long ago from associate Don Otis, who wrote me, "I still remember you telling me that you read books at stoplights! I'm not sure how that works, but I find myself carrying books . . . in lines. I hate to waste time."

Is that you too? What about when someone else is driving? If so, you can read on buses, trains, planes, monorails—even stretch limousines, if you're fortunate enough to ride in one. Hotel and resort CEO Barry Sternlight lives by this example. "I read, constantly . . . ," he has said, "when I'm on the phone, eating lunch, commuting to work and, especially, when I'm flying. I never get on a plane without a huge duffel bag full of magazines and press clippings I pile on my office floor, between long trips, plus a novel or a new design book. I pretty much spend my entire time in the air reading, and with the amount I travel, that's a lot of hours."

When I hear people say they don't have time to read, I find myself nodding in agreement with this advice from Ralph Waldo Emerson: "Guard well your spare moments. They are like uncut diamonds. Discard them, and their value will never be known. Improve them, and they will become the brightest gems in a useful life."

*We sometimes receive letters from businessmen
who say they are too busy to read. The man who
is too busy to read is never likely to read.*

—B. C. Forbes, founder of *Forbes* magazine

Will I Ever Have Read Enough?

If you're asking me, the answer is a resounding NO! And my research reveals I'm in good company. Socrates once said, "Employ your time improving yourself by other men's writings, so that you shall come easily by what others have labored hard for."

He's right! We have more books on weight loss than most other topics—when the fact is, if we just saw reading as more vital for our lives than eating, we might need the weight-loss advice less—and the world would be richer for it.

After all, what happens when you read something that inspires or challenges you? Sure, some of us close the book and go back to bed, but more people are likely to act on what they've read.

In the mid-1960s, Blanche Caffiere was a librarian at View Ridge School in Seattle. One day, a fourth-grade teacher brought in a student who kept finishing his work ahead of the class and needed more to do, something to challenge his active mind. The boy quickly picked up on the Dewey decimal classification system and became an expert shelf-stocker.

Seeing his need for an even greater challenge, Caffiere gave him a stack of cards for overdue books that had actually been returned, but misfiled. "Is it like a detective game?" the boy asked. And he was off like a bloodhound in hot pursuit. This went on for weeks, with the enterprising youth quickly rising from gofer to regular librarian.

One day, the boy's mother broke the news that the family would be moving. Both Caffiere and the boy were sad. "Who will find the lost books?" he asked.

Not long after, Caffiere was pleasantly surprised when in walked the young apprentice. "Guess what?" he said. "That other school doesn't let boys work in the library." He'd asked for and received a transfer back to View Ridge.

"I should have had an inkling that such focused determination would take that young man wherever he wanted to go," Caffiere wrote in the *Christian Science Monitor*. "What I could not have guessed, however, was that he would become a wizard of the Information Age." That boy, his active mind inspired by the world of books, grew up to be quite an entrepreneur. Today, Microsoft founder Bill Gates is one of the most successful men of all time—largely because he knew how to use his time well.

If no other book you've read has made that kind of difference for you, let this be the one book. If through this book you are convinced that reading matters, both for you and for your family—if you begin today to make books a regular, scheduled part of your day—I'll have achieved my purpose. And nothing excites me more than changed lives. Books have that kind of power.

Want to find time to read? Fall in book love.
Seek out the books that fire your passions.
Follow your intellect and your heart.
Then time will find you.

—Steve Leveen, from Starbucks' "The Way I See It" series, #94

Tips to Make Reading a Daily Decision

Motivator Brian Tracy is a man after my own heart. He challenges people everywhere to "read at least one hour per day . . . One hour a day will translate into approximately one book a week. One book a week will translate into approximately fifty books over the next twelve months. If you read an hour a day, one book per week, you will be an expert in your field within three years. You will be a national authority in five years, and you will be an international authority in seven years."

Wherever I go, whenever I speak, I deliver the same anthem. As I said a few pages ago, I challenge everyone—and that means *you*—to read, in a book, for one hour every day. Not sure it works? Try it out. Test it for a month. We'll look a little closer at this challenge later on, but for right now, hear me out. I want you to think about this.

Let's say you want to be a writer. Get yourself a stack of books on various aspects of writing and make a plan to read one hour a day as you whittle down that stack. By the end of a month, you'll know more than you did at the beginning. By the end of the year, you'll be an expert on understanding what it takes to be a great writer. Of course, you still have to apply what you've read, but you'll be amazed at how reading shapes your ideas. When you sit down with that pad of paper and pen, or roll your chair up to the computer keyboard, you'll be dazzled at the words spilling forth from your little cranium—all because you've been exercising your mind. It's as if your mind is the muscle (which it is) and the books are the weights you lift to keep that muscle in shape.

Friends, I really can't urge you enough to make reading a regular, critical part of your daily pattern. One hour, if you can—and you *can*! Try it. Be amazed at the results.

To be a reader is to think like Thomas Jefferson, who wrote to John Adams in 1815, "I cannot live without books." It is to find books as fulfilling as your life's work. Are you getting the message? It's not about *finding* time at all! It's about *making time count*—by filling it with books.

6

How to Choose Reading
When Everything Else
Is Screaming Louder

There's no doubt about it: this twenty-first-century world is full of more choices for ways to spend our minutes here on Earth than ever before in history. And it's only going to get better—or worse—depending on how you look at it. Almost all of these choices are great, fun things to do. Ask my friends and family, and they'll tell you I don't miss many opportunities to take in a great basketball or baseball game. In fact, I love all sports. But there's a big difference between a pastime and an investment of time. Yes, we all need to relax. We all need to escape from time to time and get away from the pressures of daily living. May I be bold enough to suggest that books offer both a great escape *and* a great investment of time?

When it comes to convenience, almost all the choices today are also portable—from MP3 players to DVD players for your car to laptop computers with wireless Internet connections. Books have *always* been portable—and today you can even download them to your personal data-management devices. The problem is, books don't make noise, and everything else does. As a father of nineteen, I know full well that the noisy kid gets attention first—either for good or for bad.

And then there are those movies we talked about a few pages ago. Why choose a book over a movie? Consider this: movies, while they are an amazing art form and offer their own unique cultural contributions (some more debatable than others), are really not the best way to get the whole story. After all, in a theater, you are virtually held prisoner for two hours or more. You come out of the theater, and maybe you'll discuss the film for a few minutes at dinner with your friends . . . then it's basically forgotten. Books, on the other hand, offer time to process the words, actions, and thoughts at your own speed.

In today's movies, those scenes move by our eyes pretty fast. I read recently that the average scene is less than ten seconds— not much time to think about what's going on. But with books, you can pause for a while and consider what's going on. You get to curl up inside the mind of the author, to understand what she is thinking and feeling, to connect with his life experiences. Movies are wonderful for helping us see the location, visualize the characters, and sense, for that two-hour time frame, that we are part of the action. But books flesh out the experience. They complete it, enrich it, make it whole.

It has always been my hope that
our fairy-tale films will result in a desire . . .
to read again the fine, old original tales
and enchanting myths on the home
bookshelf or school library.
Our . . . productions are
designed to augment them,
not to supplant them.

—Walt Disney

No matter what the book—fiction or nonfiction, contemporary or classic—you'll get more out of reading the words, making actual face contact with the pages, than you'll ever get out of that same time spent on almost any other personal pursuit.

Motivational speaker Fred Smith thinks, "Better to read . . . books [by interesting people] than to talk with them, for their writing is more carefully thought out than their casual conversation could ever be."

For those of us whose goal is to get others reading more, it's going to take some creative thinking to help them make this choice. Take the case of a teacher featured in the *Orange County (California) Register,* for example. Candy Mack teaches science to middle-school students. While reading is not her primary focus, reading is fundamental to her topic, as it is to understanding anything. By offering her students activities that make learning relevant to them at their age level—things like mock courtroom dramas to understand the elements of bonding, publishing their own versions of popular magazines, or a using a cooking channel segment to illustrate the principles of stable compounds—she's found a successful formula for relating to her students. They're learning and enjoying it.

Read When You Feel Powerless

We've all known moments when we were faced with a crisis, or knew someone else in a dire circumstance—and we just didn't know what to do. Those times happen in all our lives. Now I'm not saying a book will call the auto club for you if your car breaks down, but being a bookworm, believe it or not, is a powerful lifestyle choice.

"Man reading should be man intensely alive," said the late American poet Ezra Pound. "The book should be a ball of light in one's hand." What image does that idea bring to your mind? A glowing ball of power, like something in the hands of Gandalf the Grey? A crystal ball to see the future?

None of us will ever know precisely what tomorrow holds, but those of us who read books and engage in the active exchange of ideas are often the ones who shape the future. Books are building blocks, but they only work when we choose to use them.

In books lies the soul of the whole Past Time; the articulate, inaudible voice of the Past, when the body and material substance of it has altogether vanished like a dream.

—Thomas Carlyle

Read When You Have a Need

And what about those times when we need advice or comfort or friendship—but all the lines are busy? During those moments, books are the ideal soft shoulder, the perfect pal. They are there when we need them, with no demands that we return the favor. As French political thinker Charles de Secondat once noted, "I've never known any trouble that an hour's reading didn't assuage."

Never before in history have there been so many self-help books available. Whatever is troubling you, there's a book to help you get to the bottom of your blues. And if an answer isn't exactly what you're looking for, a cup or two of *Chicken Soup* is sure to help you feel better.

Nineteenth-century American poet James Russell Lowell was speaking to us today when he said, "Books are the bees which carry the quickening pollen from one to another mind." In like manner, when we're in need of answers, there are plenty of books out there just waiting to pollinate our hungry hearts.

Consider the nonstop explosion of diet books, for example. I can't remember a time when there was not at least one leading weight-loss guru with a book, promising the solution to everyone's ideal size issues. And because our understanding of the human body and how it works continues to unfold, those books remain in demand.

Or perhaps you are a new parent with a baby that just won't stop crying. Who are you going to call at two in the morning when the screaming has left you exhausted and at the point of tears? It's a perfect time to pick up an understanding book by one of the leading child care experts. There are so many to choose from—T. Berry Brazelton, James Dobson, even the Bible.

In a *Newsday* article about New York Giants general manager Ernie Accorsi, sports columnist Johnette Howard accurately captured the helplessness we GMs often feel once the season has started and the teams must live and move with our decisions. She cited a moment when my old friend Ernie confessed to me, "Pat, I want to retire. I can't take the games anymore."

"Do what I do," I told him sympathetically. "I go to the weight room. Check on the game. Go to my office. Peek at the score. Sometimes I even read a book."

Accorsi muttered something in return about not having enough games in the season for a book—but that's only because he didn't know about my speed-reading advice. At any rate, I know Accorsi gets the message, for he once said, "To me, the smarter you are, the more you want to learn."

You may not be a pro sports executive, but we all know what it is to feel stressed. And I can tell you from firsthand experience, books are great tension relievers!

In August 2000, University of Virginia women's basketball coach Debbie Ryan was diagnosed with pancreatic cancer. In the early stages of her battle, a cousin gave her Lance Armstrong's inspirational book, *It's Not About the Bike* (Berkley Trade, 2001), in which the champion describes his skirmishes and victories over cancer. "I read it cover to cover the first day," Ryan told *USA Today* (July 25, 2005), "stayed up all night."

Now cancer-free, Ryan explains the power of that book at such a critical time in her life: "When you're a cancer survivor, it's about knowing there are other people out there who have done it so you can feel like you can do it. Reading his situation and knowing how grave mine was, it gave me so much motivation and hope. It's indescribable."

Whatever your need of the moment, the first thing you need to know is that you're not alone. Now is the time to find that life partner, your own Lance Armstrong, to help you feel like you can do it. It's more than likely you'll find that hope, as Debbie Ryan did, in a book.

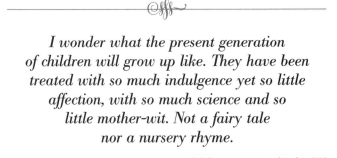

I wonder what the present generation of children will grow up like. They have been treated with so much indulgence yet so little affection, with so much science and so little mother-wit. Not a fairy tale nor a nursery rhyme.

—C. S. Lewis, writing to a friend in 1935

Read When You're Stuck on "Same"

The right books are like crowbars for our imaginations. When we find ourselves stuck at some place in life, the right book can pry open our inner idea banks. You know those moments: life has become so routine you could do it in your sleep—in fact, you wish you could. You need a change, but you're not sure if it calls for a career switch, a life overhaul, or just a new hairstyle.

During these seasons, the right book challenges you to think differently, to see life in a new light, to bring resolution to a problem, or make a life-changing decision. Books can propel you out of life's occasional ruts. Through their mind-expanding, heart-swelling, pulse-quickening words and ideas, books become like WD-40 for our brains.

Have you ever had one of those crises you wish you could talk to someone about, if you only knew who that someone could be? Books can be that someone. It's not quite the same as a two-way conversation . . . but in a way, it is. You go to the book with your questions, and then you listen as the author provides answers, advice, wisdom, or at least a few laughs to get you through the rough spots.

Early twentieth-century author Franz Kafka wrote, "I think we ought to only read the kind of books that wound and stab us. If the book we are reading doesn't wake us up with a blow on the head, what are we reading it for? . . . A book must be the axe for the frozen sea inside us." These words may seem a little harsh, but Kafka makes his point well. In some way, the books we read need to set our feet in a new direction. Isn't that what we're after?

The *When* Factor: So What Can I Do About It?

Albert Schweitzer, the famous missionary physician and winner of the Nobel Peace Prize, would sleep only four hours a night. He blamed it on his insatiable desire to read. The same was true of Mary Lyon, founder of Mount Holyoke College in Massachusetts. So "hungry" was she to devote time to reading that she deliberately ate her meals as fast as she could and slept but four hours a night. While you don't have to make such extreme choices, there are many ways to make reading a priority in your day.

1. **Decide to make reading a part of your daily life from now on.** Take out your Franklin, open your Outlook or whatever your scheduling tool of choice is, and identify a space for reading. It might mean getting up a little earlier or staying up a little later. Don't fret about the lost sleep—you

really won't miss it. You *will* miss the benefit of the books you don't read. So make that decision today—right now!

2. **Plan your reading.** Now that you've set aside a time, make a list of books you want to read. If you don't know the titles yet, just write down what kinds of books you're interested in.

Steve Leveen, author of *The Little Guide to Your Well-Read Life*, suggests developing a "List of Candidates" as a way around the more obligatory-sounding "reading list." Candidates, after all, are prospects vying for the position you have open. They're competitors who must prove they are worthy of your time and resources. Such a tactic is certainly worth considering as you plan your reading approach.

However you do it, get started. I've learned that unplanned activities are usually undone before they ever begin. It's like saying to the old friend you've just run into, "Let's get together sometime!" or the Christmas card you mail with the sincerely felt wishes, "Hoping to see more of you this year." Be honest—if you don't put it on your calendar, it won't happen.

3. **Get into the habit of taking a book along wherever you go.** That way, when those spare moments present themselves, you're ready to put them to good use. Keep one in the car, right next to you for those traffic-light moments. Put one in your briefcase to read as you wait at the airport or train station, or keep one in your car for those times when you're stuck in a parking lot waiting for the traffic jams to clear out. Keep one in your hand, if possible. It might be hard to remember at first, but once the reading bug bites you, it won't be long before you'll own the urgency. You won't need to be reminded.

4. **Develop a reader's mind-set.** Have you noticed that most things only happen when we determine to do them?

That desire needs to be more than just a wish before it will happen. Whenever you have a spare moment or two, start asking this question: "What can I read?" Or ask, "Where's my book?" Once you mentally plant reading as your regular downtime occupation, chances are, you'll amaze even yourself with how much reading you'll accomplish.

5. **Realize that books *fill* time—they don't just pass it.** Make up your mind that books matter more than video games, movies, television programs, or just about any other time occupier. It's okay to relax—in fact, most of us need to do that more. But why just pass time when you can make it count for something? Rather than spending that time on something that's gone as soon as you use it, why not invest that time in words and ideas that last your whole lifetime? As we said in the last chapter, it's about making your time on Earth count for something. Books are a great investment of time.

*Books, I found, had the power
to make time stand still, retreat,
or fly into the future.*

—Jim Bishop, twentieth-century American journalist

6. **Remember that books connect people.** Think of the words in books as hands reaching out across time to take our hands, and let us know we are not alone. I believe that is one of the deepest needs of every human heart. Books can help fill that need, and often just when we need it most. Sometimes, though, that connection sneaks up on us. We may not even be aware of the need. It's an insight that comes along and hits us over the heart when we least

expect it. Have you ever had an experience like that? Those words become the lines you remember and quote effortlessly because they are woven into the fabric of who you are. They are knitted into your soul. When it happens, when those words come along and they take your breath away, you know you've made a friend for life.

Actor and playwright Alan Bennett put it this way, "The best moments in reading are when you come across something—a thought, a feeling, a way of looking at things—which you had thought unique and particular to you. Now here it is, set down by someone else, a person you have never met, someone even who is long dead. And it is as if a hand has come out and taken yours."

7. **Recognize books as friends who are always there.** How often have you found yourself in a moment of crisis, at a crossroads where you needed the advice of a wise navigator, only to find that everyone you knew was otherwise occupied? But the right book can be just the shoulder you need. Or you might want a refresher course in something you *know* you know, but can't quite recall. With books, you don't need to wait for class to be called to session. They are your ready reference tools. Oswald Chambers once observed that books are "standing counselors and preachers, always at hand, and always disinterested; having this advantage over oral instructors, that they are ready to repeat their lesson as often as we please."

Bottom line: why does it matter that we use our time wisely? I couldn't have answered this question better than C. S. Lewis when he wrote, "Our leisure, even our play, is a matter of serious concern. There is no neutral ground in the universe: every square inch, every split second, is claimed by God and counterclaimed by Satan." Don't waste the time you've been given. It will be gone quicker than you can even imagine. Later in this book you'll read about what Andy Stanley calls "the best question ever," and this is it: *What is the wise thing for me to do today?* We never know how much time is allotted to us.

Now that you've made time in your day for books, what should you read in order to maximize your reading moments? In the next section, I'll discuss practical principles for making those choices.

Read for Your Life Way No. 5:

Discover the *Where* Factor

7

Travel the Globe–
in the Pages of a Book

When people ask me where my favorite place to read is, I answer, "Everywhere!" There is almost no place I can be found without a book in my hand. Reading is my passion—and I hope it's yours, too. If not, I trust it will be by the time you've finished this book.

I relate to Julius Pepper, star defensive end for the Carolina Panthers, who told an interviewer, "I read in my spare time, on a trip, or just around the house." I'm the same way. I "pepper" my life with a constant supply of reading material, wherever I go.

On the growing menu of portable entertainment devices, books are unique in that they build your mind, unlike many of those "other" choices that simply burn brain cells. Everywhere you go, books can go.

Better yet, books can take you anywhere you want to go. Can't afford that trip to Hawaii just yet? Read a Michener novel, and go there today.

As writer Caroline Gordon has said, "A well-composed book is a magic carpet on which we are wafted to a world that we cannot enter in any other way."

Boldly Go Where You've Never Gone Before—in a Book

Do you like to travel? Maybe your answer is, "Yes! But there's never enough time or money to go where I want to go." Well, in books you can go anywhere you want! You can even visit places no one could possibly go outside of books.

With Alice and the White Rabbit as tour guides, you could spend an afternoon in Wonderland—without having the Queen of Hearts take off your head. Or you could sprinkle on a little pixie dust and fly "second to the right—and straight on 'til morning," with Peter Pan and company.

Do you need to get away from it all? Books can take you through a wardrobe into the land of Narnia, or whisk you on board a star speeder headed for Endor or Tatooine. There are worlds to discover beyond this one! Worlds you'd never know about . . . if it weren't for books.

Yes, many of the books I'm describing have been made into movies—because great literature always begs for more! So you could "cheat" by slipping in a DVD for a couple hours, but ultimately you'd be cheating yourself. *Peter Pan* author J. M. Barrie, for example, was one of the most successful playwrights of his day because he had an amazing imagination and well-developed writing skills—and great writers deserve to be read.

---

*Some of my dearest friends have solved
murders, broken hearts, and kept entire families
going on nothing more than a wing and a prayer.
They've been seduced, corrupted, made whole,
set free, and loved like nobody's business.
Where did I meet this amazing collection of
characters? In brilliant book after book after book.*

If you can read, you can empathize, luxuriate,
take a chance, have a laugh, hit the road,
witness history, become enlightened,
turn the page, and do it all again.

—Oprah Winfrey

Movies may help introduce you to characters like Aslan or Frodo, or they can fill in details of the mental picture painted by the books. But don't let that movie experience be all the time you share with these characters. Get to know them better. Books let you climb inside a character's mind in ways no movie ever could. Explore their lives and thoughts as their creators intended, in their books. You'll be amazed at how sharing these adventures transports you into other worlds.

Thanks to the popular Harry Potter series, more kids today are reading than in "pre-Potter" years. That's encouraging. It's true these books have not been without controversy, but who can truly argue with anything that stimulates young imaginations and engages minds with words on pages?

Through books you can travel to other lands, explore other cultures, and even visit different eras in history. You can even feed future dreams!

New York Giants' running back Tiki Barber told *USA Today,* "I remember picking up *Lonesome Dove* when I was fourteen just because it was around, and I felt like I was in the Wild West." Barber was so inspired by this event that, years later, it has motivated him to write books children will read. "Get an eight-year-old boy who hates reading but picks up a book about football and learns a lesson, maybe he'll get the next one, then go on to read something else" ("Barber's Reach Expands to TV, Radio, Kids," *USA Today,* December 7, 2006).

So besides the question of where to take your books, there's the issue of where books can take you. When you're planning a trip to a brand-new destination, you're likely to visit your local bookstore and do a little research. What's the weather like? How should you dress when you're there? Is it likely to be a peaceful place, or one with lots of activity? You can find those answers before you "book" your trip, in the pages of someone's bound and published manuscript.

*In this job, there are some simple pleasures
in life that really help you cope. One is books . . .
books are a great escape. Books are a way
to get your mind on something else.*

−George W. Bush

Did you know you can learn about other places—not just travel destinations, but other lands, other cultures, other periods in history, even places that don't really exist—in books?

In *The O'Reilly Factor for Kids,* popular news analyst Bill O'Reilly described this vicarious travel plan:

I know something about your classmates . . .

Last night, one of them traveled back in time two hundred years to England and watched a pirate kidnap a young teenager and take him on a great adventure.

Another flew in a spaceship to a strange planet where there were three green suns in the daytime sky, and where giant plants curled their strong tendrils around human beings and then ate them like cheese sticks.

Still another ran away from home and hitchhiked to San Francisco to get away from a drunken father . . .

Of course, I'm talking about their reading excursions. Reading can take you into and out of a million different places. A good book can scare you or make you laugh, teach you about distant lands and times, or make you cry in sympathy for another. Or better still, a good book can help you understand who you are more clearly.

With books, just add your imagination and you can go—anywhere! Next time you feel an urge to "get away from it all," pick up a book that will take you there.

I like the way Oprah Winfrey put it when she wrote, "What I love most about reading: It gives you the ability to reach higher ground. A world of possibilities awaits you. Keep turning the page" (*O, The Oprah Magazine,* July 2006).

Read to Succeed

Do you know where you want to go in life? Research shows that there is a direct link between how much we read and how much we achieve in life. Do you want to be more tomorrow than you are today? I know I do. Paul Copperman, founder of the Institute of Reading Development, called reading "a necessity. There won't be . . . a lot of jobs in the twenty-first century for people who don't have good reading skills." A future prediction like that should get everyone's attention.

Not all readers become leaders, but all leaders must be readers.

−Harry S. Truman

Motivational speaker and leader Brian Tracy offers this advice:

Arise early, each morning, and read for thirty to sixty minutes in your field. Underline and take notes. Think of how you can apply what you are learning to your day-to-day work. Throughout the day think of how you can use what you read to be more effective. At the end of each day, review the day, based on your new knowledge and skills, and evaluate your results and progress. When you read in your field, for thirty to sixty minutes each day, and think about how you could apply what you have learned, throughout the day, you will tend to become better and better at what you do, both consciously and unconsciously. The improved results you get will accumulate and compound, over time. You will become better and better at what you do, almost without being aware of it. If you read thirty to sixty minutes, each day, you should complete about one book per week.

The average American reads less than one book per year. If you read one book per week, you should finish at least fifty books, each year. As it happens, earning a Ph.D. from a major university requires the reading and synthesis into a dissertation of about forty to fifty books.

If you were to read one book, per week, fifty books per year, you would be getting the equivalent of a practical Ph.D. in your field, each year. If you continued reading at this level . . . fifty books per year . . . you would read 500 books in the next ten years. If you were to read 500 books in your field, in a world where the average person reads less than one book per year, do you think you might gain an edge? . . .

You must discipline yourself to leave the television or radio off, to put the newspaper aside and perhaps to rise a little earlier in the morning, so you can invest in your mind. This investment will give you one of the highest payoffs in terms of results, rewards, and satisfaction that you will ever enjoy from anything you do. The average person spends 500 to 1,000 hours, each year, in his or her car. This is the equivalent of three to six months of forty-hour weeks, or the equivalent of one or two university semesters.

In fact, the University of Southern California recently concluded that we could get the equivalent of almost full-time university attendance simply by listening to educational audio programs as we drove from place to place during the course of the week.

Motivational speaker Reid Buckley once said, "If you are not continually learning and upgrading your skills, somewhere, someone else is and, when you meet that person, you will lose." Are people who read successful? Maybe not in every single case, but the reverse is definitely true: successful people are people who read. Research shows us that there is a direct link between how much we read and how much we achieve in life. Do you want to be more tomorrow than you are today? Start reading!

The *Where* Factor: So What Can I Do About It?

Publishers Weekly writer Robert Masello dug into the reading habits of the average American book buyer ("Reader as Lab Rat," June 26, 2006) and made some interesting discoveries. For example, did you know that, second only to restaurants, bookstores are the most popular place to meet a blind date? The number-one reason for reading, Masello also revealed, was escape, followed by self-improvement. So if you're there to meet a blind date, and your date isn't quite what you'd hoped for, you'll find self-improvement by escaping down one of the bookstore's numerous aisles. Here are some ideas for finding a place to read:

1. **Identify a "readin' place."** Masello's article noted that home is the most popular place for reading, so look around your house and choose a spot you think is conducive to reading. It might be your bedroom, your most comfy sofa, a big chair, or even your office. You may enjoy sitting outside in the sunshine on your patio. The point is, just as the character Br'er Rabbit in Joel Chandler Harris's classic Uncle Remus stories had his favorite "laughin' place," you need a "readin' place." Personally, I pick a straight-backed chair, one I'm careful is supportive but not too comfortable . . . because I know if I relax too much, I'll be asleep in five minutes or less.

Be creative! Charles Melcher realized that people like to read in lots of places, such as at the beach or when they're soaking in the tub. So why not make waterproof books? That's exactly what Melcher and his Melcher Media associates did through a brand called DuraBooks. Where were those when I was teaching my kids to swim?

Whether your personal choice is the beach or the bleachers, the idea is to find a regular place to read. Whatever works for you, let that space guide—but not limit—your daily reading.

There is a great deal of difference between an eager man who wants to read a book and the tired man who wants a book to read.

—G. K. Chesterton

---

2. **Picture your mind as a location.** It is, you know. In fact, it's the place where you spend most of your time. American history and military chronicler Edgar Puryear, Jr., wrote of Benjamin Franklin, "Where did his ideas originate, and how did he prepare himself for such significant positions of responsibility? The answer was that he loved to read. Franklin reflected, 'This library afforded me the means of improvement, by constant study, for which I set apart an hour or two, each day and, thus, repaired in some degree, the loss of the learned education my father once intended for me. Reading was the only amusement I allowed myself. I spent no time in tavern games, or frolics of any kind, and my industry in my business continued as indefatigable as it was necessary.'"

Ben Franklin, one of the men most responsible for the ideals upon which America is founded, clearly understood that his mind was a place. He wisely made it a reading room.

3. **Business leaders, consider a devoted space for reading in the workplace.** Influential companies like Starbucks, Microsoft, Boeing, Google, Altria, and even the United States Treasury, according to a *New York Times* report (May 16, 2006), have responded positively to programs like the one from Simon & Schuster that bring authors into companies for scheduled readings. Why not do something like that for your employees?

4. **Determine to never leave home without a book.** I travel frequently, as you might guess, and that means a lot of dining alone. But I'm never really alone because I always take a book to dinner with me. That's a great place to read. Take a book with you whenever you go out, just in case you end up without a lunch partner or get stuck waiting while a family member shops. Those semiprivate moments are great for catching a few extra pages. While traveling, don't forget to read en route. Reading on planes was noted as the third most popular venue, according to the *Publishers Weekly* article.

5. **Know where you want to go, and let books help you find the way.** Have you ever filled out a job application? One frequent question posed, either on the application or by the interviewer, is, "Where do you see yourself in five years?" I'm convinced that most of us are hard-pressed to answer that question.

My young friend Adam Witty, still in his early twenties, owns a successful media company helping speakers and authors get their start. His dynamic personality makes him a popular presenter at events all over the country. I've known Adam's family for many years, and I can honestly say I've rarely met a young man more focused than Adam. What is it that makes Adam stand above the crowd, aside from his 6'7" height? Adam learned early on the power of seeing where he would be in five years. A voracious reader, Adam understands the power of books to fill in the blanks in your dreams.

———————————— ⁓ ————————————

At the end of the day,
I am convinced that reading has
been the most important skill I have ever
acquired. Through books, I have sharpened
my mind, expanded my context of reality,
and set an ambitious course
for my road ahead.

—Adam Witty, entrepreneur

If you've ever said, "I just don't see myself doing that," then please understand the tremendous influence of a vision—of being able to see yourself doing that. Twenty-five years ago, I couldn't see myself adopting children. Today, I can only think how much poorer my life would have been had I not brought these children into my home. Once I saw myself "doing that," there was no stopping me.

Advice dispenser Fred Smith puts it this way: "Do you want to shoot for the moon, or be happy in a single-engine plane?" Why settle for less than all life has to bring your way? Books help you build your own personal dream rocket.

One last thought about where to read: I can't help but identify with the sentiments of the late author and Harvard Medical School dean, Oliver Wendell Holmes, Sr., who said: "It is a good plan to have a book with you in all places and at all times. If you are presently without, hurry without delay to the nearest shop and buy one of mine." Of course, I'm referring to the concept of having a book with you at all times, but Holmes's quip gave me a chuckle.

So when you're wondering where you can tuck reading into your life, think of that familiar credit-card ad, but with this twist: "Books—don't leave home without one."

Read for Your Life Way No. 6:

Explore the *What* Factor

8

Read Books That Illuminate Yesterday

W hen you're an avid reader like I am, the question of what to read is less likely to be one involving a search than one involving a choice. More often than not, the question I'm confronted with is not "what," but "which." When I travel—and I'm on the road a lot—the decisions I make are not related to airlines, clothes, or how long I'll be gone. The primary issue I'm faced with is what books I am taking. Generally, I take too many. Where others might be afraid of flying, my great fear is—*what if I run out of reading material? What will I do?* Serious readers never get to the end of a book and think *now what?* I've got eight or nine books going at the same time. I've got them everywhere.

About a dozen years or so ago, I got very behind on my reading. Now I estimate there are well over 250 books stacked in my home library, waiting to be read. To complicate things further, I've got new volumes coming every week! And I'm convinced these books talk to each other. It's like *Toy Story* in my library. They *know* when I'm leaving on a trip. If I take a new one, I can't leave the old one. I can hear them saying, "I want to go. When is it my turn? You keep telling me I get to go." They're like children. Every week I have to go through this!

Books were only one type of receptacle
where we stored a lot of things we were afraid
we might forget. There is nothing magical in them
at all. The magic is only in what books say, how
they stitched the patches of the universe together
into one garment for us . . . Do you know why
books such as this are so important? Because they
have quality. And what does the word quality
mean? To me it means texture. This book has
pores. It has features. This book can go under the
microscope. You'll find life under the glass,
streaming past in infinite profusion.

—Professor Faber to Fireman Montag, in *Fahrenheit 451*

I'll concede the point: there are *so many* books out there and *only* so much time. Where does a person who wants to read begin? Why not take Professor Faber's advice—go for quality. Choose books that enhance your life, build your character, inspire your mind—books that can take microscopic scrutiny and live to tell about it, over and over. CNN's Anderson Cooper has said, "The mark of a good book is it changes every time you read it." I would add that a good book changes *you* every time you read it. Readers understand that. They've witnessed the process over and over.

Not long ago, I had an opportunity to appear on a television program to discuss the book of that moment. After the taping, as I was waiting for a ride back to the hotel, I made small talk with the producer.

"So Pat," she asked, "what's next?" I told her about this book on reading, and that was all it took to make the connection. "Oh!" she said. "I love to read. I read as much as I can. In fact, my husband knows when I'm not reading."

"How is that?" I asked.

"Well, when I'm not reading, bad stuff comes out of my mouth," she explained. "It's that old programming thing. If I'm reading good stuff and putting good programming into my mind, good things come out of my mouth. When I'm not reading, he knows immediately." So you see, books literally have the power to change us!

Philosopher and eighteenth-century author Samuel Johnson recommended reading books you enjoy. "A man ought to read just as inclination leads him," Johnson said, "for what he reads as a task will do him little good." While we're in school, it's sad but often true that we're required to read books that do not hold our interest. That's unfortunate for many reasons. Boring books, encountered one time too often, can give birth to the notion that *all* books are boring—but this is simply not true.

If you're in that place where you *must* read about topics that don't engage your mind, or you're required to read books written in a style that leaves you crying for mercy, l urge you to find another book to read for fun. Once you've finished your daily assignment, clean your mental palate, so to speak, from that dry book you had to choke down with words that refresh and restore your soul. I love books, as you can tell. But even I will admit that not all books are good books.

[The hobbits] like to have books filled with things that they already knew, set out fair and square with no contradictions.

—J. R. R. Tolkien, *The Lord of the Rings*

So start with books that interest you.

And by the way, when it comes to making those decisions, Fred Smith offers this wise advice: "I wear glasses, and maybe you do, too. Mine probably cost about the same as yours. Would you trade lenses with me just because I asked you to? Of course not! That would be silly because yours fit you and mine fit me. Reading is the same thing. Are you reading what the boss is reading, or are you reading what fits you? Are you reading a book because someone sent it to you? How about because it is on the bestseller list? You wouldn't wear someone else's glasses—don't let them pick your books. Understand what your purpose is for reading and carefully discipline your choices."

Now that we've got that established, let's narrow the field a little.

Choose Books That Remind You of Your Place in Time

Your life is not an isolated moment in time. You are part of history, connected to those around you, to those who've gone before and to those yet to come. Books are the alloy that helps solder those connections.

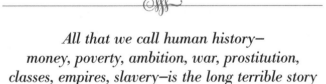

All that we call human history—
money, poverty, ambition, war, prostitution,
classes, empires, slavery—is the long terrible story
of man trying to find something other than
God which will make him happy.

—C. S. Lewis

In spite of our tendency to move on to the next trend, to consider that which has passed from momentary favor as "*so* yesterday," the fact is that we are part of yesterday. Yesterday is a part of us. The same is true of today, and of tomorrow. Because we are here now, we are part of time, for all time.

There's an old saying that goes something like this: "Those who fail to learn from history are doomed to repeat it." Have you ever found yourself listening to a leader, whether in business or politics, expounding on some plan to change the future—only to think to yourself, *But we already tried that!* It's frustrating, but true. We seem at times to be hopelessly done in by short-term memory problems. I can't count how many times I've heard my kids say, "Aw, Dad, you're so old-fashioned," when I counsel them regarding a road I see them heading down. Maybe you've heard it, too, or even said it. "That was *so* long ago!" they continue. "Times have changed."

Times may change, but people don't.

The hopes and dreams you cherish are largely the same as mine. This has been the case since people first showed up on the Earth. We all desire to be loved for who we are; we crave acceptance; we all long to be free. And most of us do at least one or two foolish things along the way in our desire to meet those needs. Why does it so often take a lifetime to realize that unconditional love is a gift that must be freely given, not a prize to be won? How can we know these critical truths, especially when most of us won't listen to our "old-fashioned" parents?

We can learn them from books. While I admit my first choices are current books, I recognize and appreciate the value of books published decades ago, even centuries ago. In their pages, we find thoughts, ideas, cherished hopes that are our own today. "Wow!" I've heard more than one college student exclaim, "That Shakespeare fella thinks a lot like I do!" or "People did those things back when Chaucer was alive? That's just like now!" Pardon me for stating the obvious here, but—well, duh! The folks at Microsoft and Macintosh may be continually updating their operating systems, but people work on the same "software" as they always have. People do not change.

Hope for America's future is embedded in her past. Do you know

America's history? How well do you understand the principles upon which this great nation was built? There are so many voices out there today, claiming to speak for our values . . . but what are those values, really? What is it that makes America distinctly America?

You can learn about it through good history books. Let them grow your understanding of why America came to be, what her early values were, who her first leaders were, and what mattered most to them. If we fail to learn these lessons, we may just lose what our Founding Fathers fought so hard to gain. Current indicators show we're headed there already. I don't know about you, but that thought makes my heart ache.

The only right way of learning the science of war is to read and reread the campaigns of the great generals.

—Napoleon Bonaparte

I encourage you, my friend, to be part of the solution. It's not too late to reverse the trend. Rescue America's tomorrow by knowing her history. When we understand where we came from and why, both our present and our future make so much more sense.

There are so many great books about America's history—from biographies of our Founding Fathers and inspiring leaders to firsthand reports to chronicled histories and analytical accounts. Books illuminate the past in ways that just could change tomorrow. As British statesman Benjamin Disraeli once said, "The more extensive a man's knowledge of what has been done, the greater will be his power of knowing what to do."

9

Read Books That Illustrate Today

No matter how long we live or how many books we read, we will *still* never know everything. The good news is, no matter how much you know today, you *can* know more before this day is over. Even old dogs, or so the evidence says, *can* learn new tricks.

Books give us a window into the knowledge that others have invested lifetimes to learn. In that way, books are like information shortcuts. Better yet, they help us envision our life's destinations. They illustrate our dreams.

Walt Disney was big on "plussing" his products—taking what was already good and adding detail to make it just a little bit better. Think of books as your personal "plus" factor.

What do you want to learn about? Are you a young person with big dreams? Books can help you refine, name, and explore those dreams. Read biographies of people you admire. The life stories of legends often inspire us to rise above obstacles that might otherwise discourage us from succeeding. Read some of the many books available today by gurus who are living your dream. Then add to the mix those unique natural ingredients that make you who you are and do them one better. I've been fortunate to know many successful people in my long career. I can't think of one of them whose life was not "plussed" by reading books about people they wanted to be like.

If you only read what you agree with,
you'll never learn anything.

—James D. Hodgson, former U.S. secretary of labor

At the tender age of eleven, young Ewing Marion Kauffman found himself facing a life-threatening illness that left him bedridden for months. During that time, his mother brought him library books to read—a dozen a week. He read biographies of presidents, frontiersmen, and others he admired. He even read the Bible twice. Young Ewing survived that illness and went on to become the man who founded the Marion Laboratories global health company and who took the Kansas City Royals from an expansion team to a world championship team in just sixteen years (1968–85). He was inspired by the lives of great leaders he read about as a boy. Where could a book take you?

Are you at the bottom rung of your career ladder? Books offer advice from those who've gone before you. Just think of the mistakes you don't have to make, simply by learning from someone else's. As Anne Shirley, heroine of Lucy Maud Montgomery's Anne of Green Gables series, might say, "Each day is like a clean sheet of paper, with no mistakes in it yet." As a young professional, you have the benefit of fewer mistakes to tarnish your reputation. Let someone else's mistakes be your shortcut to avoiding future pitfalls. Yes, you're still going to make plenty of your own. They seem to be a necessary part of life—like pain. We can't know what pleasure feels like until we've known hurt. And we can't know the right way to go until we've made a few wrong turns. But learning how others before you have traveled the road can help you steer clear of a lot of unmarked sharp turns and dangerous curves. Books are like portable mentors—and you can "do lunch" with them anytime you like.

Success trainer Brian Tracy observes that the adult brain "is designed so that you only learn and remember something if it is immediately relevant and applicable to your current situation. No matter how interesting it might be, if you cannot connect the information to your current life work situation, and visualize how you might apply the idea immediately, it will slip through your mind, like water through a grate, and you will not remember it at all.

"For this reason," Tracy advises, "you should not waste time reading subjects that may be of interest to you 'someday.'"

Choose Books That Challenge You to Change Your World

Do you have a desire to change the world you live in? No matter what your age, career status, or present life season, books can help define your vision—and vision is one of the first keys of leadership.

For my book *Coaching Your Kids to Be Leaders* (Warner Faith, 2005), I interviewed Reverend Bruce Chesser, pastor of Geyer Springs First Baptist Church in Little Rock, Arkansas. He had this to say about vision: "The Bible tells us, 'Where there is no vision, the people perish.' The word for 'perish' can also be translated 'lose control.' People need visionary leadership at every level—in the home, in the church, in the nation. An organization or society without a vision—and without a leader to articulate that vision—is in big trouble. A lack of visionary leadership produces chaos. That is why young people need to step up, dream their dreams for a brighter future, and become leaders and proponents for those dreams. Without a vision, without leadership, our organizations and our society will be out of control; they will perish."

The books which help you most
are those which make you think the most.
The hardest way of learning is by easy reading:
but a great book that comes from a great thinker—
it is a ship of thought, deep freighted
with truth and with beauty.

—Theodore Parker,
nineteenth-century theologian and thinker

Do you care what happens tomorrow? I'm betting you do, or you wouldn't be reading this book. People who read are people who care. That makes you a leader! Read books that inspire your vision. Be a part of making tomorrow better for everyone who lives it. Books open our eyes to current world problems; books open our hearts to want solutions; and books open our minds to see the answers.

And one final thought on leadership: if you're a leader, don't neglect the care and feeding of those under your management. Make sure they are reading, too. Try to build reading time into their work schedules, at least for books that help them do their jobs more productively. Then encourage them to read on their own. Better yet, set the example.

Give attendance to reading,
to exhortation, to doctrine.

—The Apostle Paul
(1 Timothy 4:13, KJV)

Choose Books That Ask the Right Questions

Here in twenty-first-century America, we're surrounded by so much entertainment, noise, and busyness that we find ourselves, all too often, living on the surface of life.

Whatever questions we had when we were kids, many of us have stopped asking. It's not that the answers aren't out there; it's just that we're too busy to look for them right now. Or maybe it's easier to look the other way.

So we pass our lives with pleasant exchanges: "How you doin'?" "Have a nice day!" "What's up?" or even "God bless you." But do we really want to know how that acquaintance is doing? Do we care about "what's up?" How sincere are we being when we toss off these casual, socially acceptable comments? How long has it been since you had a real conversation with another person, one that went deeper than the events of the day? How long has it been since you even asked yourself what life is all about? Could we be closer to Guy Montag's world than we know?

"Are you happy?" [Clarisse] said.
"Am I what?" [Montag] cried.
But she was gone—running in the moonlight . . .
"Happy! Of all the nonsense."
He stopped laughing.
"Of course I'm happy. What does she think?
I'm not?" he asked the quiet rooms.

—from Ray Bradbury's *Fahrenheit 451*

Today, faith-based books top the bestseller lists and smile out at you from almost every bookstore display. That tells me we really *do* want to know if we're happy, or how to be happy—or whether or not happiness is even a worthwhile, attainable goal.

Not that long ago, books by such popular authors as Joel Osteen, Tim LaHaye, and Rick Warren wouldn't be found outside a Christian bookstore. Yet today they are the leaders of the pack, and that's a good sign.

Every man who knows how to read has it in his power to magnify himself, to multiply the ways in which he exists, to make his life full, significant, and interesting.

—Aldous Huxley, author

A recent *New York Times* book review ("Faith-Based Publishing," by Rachel Donadio) quoted a Rick Warren e-mail. "Something really big is happening, but it has been happening under the radar of the national media. They've missed it entirely . . . we're at the beginning of a New Reformation," Warren wrote, "that will inevitably affect everyone else." Pointing to the success of Warren's *The Purpose Driven Life* (Zondervan, 2002), read primarily in small-group contexts, the article observed, "There is certainly something compelling about a group of people being on the same page." Religious books, according to this report, currently represent 11 percent of trade sales. If Warren is right, we all need to be honest with ourselves about what matters most in life.

Read books that help you remember the questions.

And speaking of questions . . .

Ask Yourself the Best Question Ever

On January 31, 2006, I had the privilege of addressing an audience of middle-schoolers in Dorchester, Massachusetts, on the occasion of the late, great Jackie Robinson's eighty-seventh birth-day. After outlining five great lessons of Robinson's life, I encouraged the kids to always ask themselves this question: *What is the wise thing for me to do today?*

That question came from a book by Andy Stanley, founding pastor of North Point Community Church in Alpharetta, Georgia. When *The Best Question Ever* came out in 2004, I was so impressed with it that I bought two cases. It's a tiny book—less than one hundred pages—but it's a gem. I gave it to all my children, my coworkers, their spouses, and my friends. It's about foolproofing your future. Every time you need to make a decision, Stanley wrote, first ask yourself that question, the best question ever: *What is the wise thing for me to do today?*

If you'll remember to ask yourself that question every day, at the beginning of the day, you'll live a far more satisfied life. I'm grateful to Stanley for writing that book . . . and to all the other authors whose books play such a huge role in answering that question.

Choose Books That Give Us the Answers

Do you admire, as I do, people who always seem to know just what to do, no matter what? Some people are naturally gifted with self-confidence, but most of us only know what to do by experience. One way to get that experience is through books. As I said earlier, books let us learn through other people's lives.

One area where I believe we're all going to need answers in the near future is in health care. As the options become increasingly more complex and the information more difficult to wade through, managing our own health-care options is essential.

One of the breakout books of the early 2000s was *You: The Owner's Manual* (Michael F. Roizen and Mehmet C. Oz, Harper-Resources)—a book that helps ordinary people like you and me understand basic body mechanics. "People are worried," wrote Natalie Danford for *Publishers Weekly* (June 27, 2005), referring to the current health-care environment. "Health-care consumers are well-advised to educate themselves about health and disease . . ." We can do some of that research online or from magazines, but books written by experts offer an on-hand resource for answers. Books like these help us make informed decisions about our futures, decisions that may deeply impact the lives of our loved ones as well.

---

*While attending seminary,
Martin Luther King, Jr., read extensively
in the areas of history, philosophy, and religion.
With each book and each discipline, he questioned
what he truly believed. As he read, learned,
and reflected, he molded his values and
vision on the anvil of discovery.*

—Wayne Hastings and Ron Potter, leadership experts

Adam Morrison of the Charlotte Bobcats is known to consume as many as three books a week. What's less known about this talented player involves his lifelong battle with type 1 diabetes. Naturally, for this avid reader, that's one of the topics Morrison has thoroughly researched. When people challenge him regarding diabetics making it in professional sports, Morrison comes right back with answers about other athletes who've succeeded in spite of diabetes. He has books to thank for that confidence.

Books have the capacity to do something so amazing that it's almost supernatural: they can meet us in our need, care for us in our time of crisis. In 1982, I found myself in one of those places. My marriage was in huge trouble. We men can get so caught up in making a living and in doing all the "stuff" that makes us feel like warriors that life slips past us, and that's where I found myself. Women, you ask what it takes to get men to read marriage books?

In a word: desperation. When my wife shut down on me emotionally, I panicked. I was ready to do anything to fix the problem. That's when I discovered the answers I needed—in a book. Written by Dr. Ed Wheat, *Love Life for Every Married Couple* (Zondervan, 1980) met me at the exact place where I needed help, and at just the right moment.

[Books] are for company the best friends,
in Doubt's Counsellors, in Damps Comforters,
Time's Perspective the Home Traveller's Ship or
Horse, the busie Man's best Recreation,
the Opiate of idle Weariness, the Mindes
best Ordinary, Nature's Garden and
Seed-plot of Immortality.

—Bulstrode Whitelocke, seventeenth-century scholar
[Note: Because Whitelocke left behind a detailed diary, historians have great insight into British political and scholarly life of that era.]

That little 287-page classic helped me see what I'd been missing. It absolutely, for the first time, gave me a clear picture of what it takes to be a good husband. I thought I knew, but I didn't. Dr. Wheat took four letters, B.E.S.T., and made an acrostic: **B**lessing, **E**difying, **S**haring, and **T**ouching. Those were the foundations of a successful marriage. Until that book came into my life, I just didn't grasp that.

Today, when I meet men who happen to be where I was—and I recognize that look on their faces, believe me—I know I've got someone on my hands who is teachable, very receptive, very frantic. That's when I tell them, "You need to get Dr. Wheat's book!" And they can't wait to get it. Today, there are at least eight zillion marriage books out there, but I don't know of one more pertinent or more effective than that one. It's still in print, and it's the best one I know.

My point here is not to sell you a book on marriage, necessarily—although if you need one, you now have my number-one recommendation—but I want you to see that books are a far better choice, when you need answers, expert advice, or tips from someone who's been there, than so many of the ultimately empty options out there.

Books not only give you answers, but they can literally change your life.

Football great Ernie Accorsi, former general manager of the New York Giants, Baltimore Colts, and Cleveland Browns, is a good friend of mine. When asked what got him started as an NFL executive, Accorsi said, "I grew up in Hershey, Pennsylvania, and loved sports. I always followed the Philadelphia teams. In 1957, a book came out about Branch Rickey, the great baseball executive, written by Arthur Mann. I saw the book at the Hershey library, read it—and it changed my life. After reading that book, I made a decision about what to do with my career." Ernie was a class behind me at Wake Forest, so I'm guessing he was about sixteen when he read that book—which, by the way, I discovered is still in my library as well.

The power of books to influence our lives is a value recognized as long ago as the sixteenth century, when Renaissance scholar Michel de Montaigne observed, "I love such books as are either easy and entertaining, and that tickle my fancy, or such as give me comfort, and offer counsel in reordering my life and death."

Thanks to that marvelous fifteenth-century invention—the printing press—we are blessed today to have books on almost any topic that teases, torments, or perplexes us.

10

Read Books
That Inform Tomorrow

Great books can be turning points in our lives. Through books we might discover the answers to mysteries that haunt us, comprehend issues that taunt us, or catch up and even surpass those who flaunt their greatness at us.

As I mentioned previously, when I was a youngster, a book called *Pop Warner's Book for Boys* dramatically impacted my life. That book profoundly influenced the man I would later become simply by setting standards—by telling me what a real, professional athlete looked like. As I would later discover, it turned out to be a less-than-accurate picture, but that was the point. He wasn't trying to show reality at all. Pop Warner offered the ideal. And isn't that what we're all looking for?

Three other books became turning points at various stages of my life, and I'll get to all of them before our time together is up. My goal is that you fully grasp the enormous, life-changing power of books!

---

*I read as if time were running out,
because technically it is. As I grow older I find
I'm increasingly impatient with mediocre
entertainments: I want books that will take my
breath away and realign my vision.*

—Barbara Kingsolver, novelist

Young John Grisham had a high-school English teacher, Frances McGuffey, of all names, who assigned her class to read Steinbeck's *Tortilla Flats*. Grisham confessed, "I sneaked back into her room to say I liked it. I was a jock in a clique with other jocks, and you weren't supposed to go out of your way to talk to teachers." Clearly, Grisham had been hooked by what he read if he was willing to "break training" and actually talk to his teacher about it. So it was reading the work of a great writer that changed the life of John Grisham, inspiring him to become a great writer, too.

If the thought of reading great writing flutters your eyelids, but you're not quite sure where to start, here are a few ideas.

The Classics

I'll confess that fiction is not my personal first choice. In fact, I've been known to agree with Mark Twain, who once opined, "A classic is something that everybody wants to have read and nobody wants to read."

But I recognize the value of classic works of literature. Rich with universal themes and lessons, these great works bear ideas that transcend time. It goes back to that idea of personal perspective we talked about earlier. Classic works of literature help us see that people in every era of history wrestled with the same questions we face today. We are not alone in time. Books connect us to our past.

It's as if they reach across the span of time itself, like one who stands in the gap, linking today with yesterday and tomorrow.

Every page allows me to live in
[the main character's] thoughts and marvel
at how all of us who grew up poor and female are
bonded, regardless of where we were raised or
who raised us. I not only feel I know this person,
but I also recognize more of myself.
That's just one of the great joys of reading.
Insight, escape, information, knowledge, power.
All that and more can come through a good book
. . . If you're going to binge, literature
is definitely the way to do it.

—Oprah Winfrey
(*O, The Oprah Magazine*, July 2006)

Fiction, so its readers tell me, has the power to take us out of ourselves and put us into another world, into someone else's life, as it were. The worst of it at least offers momentary escape from real-world pressures and tensions. But the best of it does so much more. Great fiction transports us into other realms. It takes us into those other worlds we've always known existed outside this one. And by taking us out of this world for a time, we identify with the hero's journey. We, like the protagonist, are transformed by the characters we've met and the problems we've faced in life. The choices made in great novels are based on situations we all encounter at some time and in some way. So when we return to "normal," when we close the book and rejoin life, we often find fresh courage and reinforced wisdom for the choices we must make. Like Wendy, our time spent in Neverland reminds us of the need to hold on to childlike hopes and dreams as we face the terror of growing up. And that thought *still* terrifies me!

In his short scholarly work, *An Experiment in Criticism*, Professor C. S. Lewis wrote: "Literature enlarges our being by admitting us to experiences not our own . . . Those of us who have been true readers all our lives seldom realize the enormous extension of our being that we owe to authors. We realize it best when we talk with an unliterary friend. He may be full of goodness and good sense, but he inhabits a tiny world. In it, we should be suffocated. My own eyes are not enough for me . . . In reading great literature I become thousand men and yet remain myself . . . Here, as in worship, in love, in moral action, and in knowing, I transcend myself: and am never more myself than when I do."

Author Orson Scott Card poses this provocative question: "Why else do we read fiction, anyway? Not to be impressed by somebody's dazzling language—or at least I hope that's not our reason. I think that most of us, anyway, read these stories that we know are not 'true' because we're hungry for another kind of truth: the mythic truth about human nature in general, the particular truth about those life-communities that define our own identity, and the most specific truth of all: our own self-story. Fiction, because it is not about somebody who actually lived in the real world, always has the possibility of being about ourselves."

Professor Lewis, who was one of the twentieth century's most influential thinkers and writers, also made this observation about classic literature: "This mistaken preference for the modern books and this shyness of the old ones is nowhere more rampant than in theology. Wherever you find a little study circle of Christian laity, you can be almost certain that they are studying not St. Luke or St. Paul or St. Augustine . . . " Instead, Lewis said, they would be reading the contemporary writers. The same is true today. But why is this so? Lewis went on to say, "Now this seems to me topsy-turvy. Naturally, since I myself am a writer, I do not wish the ordinary reader to read no modern books. But if he must read only the new or only the old, I would advise him to read the old."

Lewis is right, of course. The great truths of life rise to greater heights when we see them magnified in the pages of past time. But why not read both? Why not make a daily reading list that includes a little classical and a little contemporary writing? As a student of the Bible, I've observed that reading the New Testament sheds light on the Old. I believe it is like that with reading anything. We need both the old, the classic works of literature, and contemporary books—just as we need relationships with people who are both older and younger than ourselves. To achieve a well-rounded perspective on life, we need the wisdom of age and the enthusiasm of youth, balanced on either side of now.

The Bible

On January 25, 1945, at the height of World War II, a special edition of the New Testament was distributed to millions of soldiers. President Franklin D. Roosevelt himself had written the prologue, which read:

"To the Armed Forces: As Commander-in-Chief, I take pleasure in commending the reading of the Bible to all who serve in the armed forces of the United States.

"Throughout the centuries men of many faiths and diverse origins have found in the Sacred Book words of wisdom, counsel, and inspiration.

"It is a fountain of strength and now, as always, an aid in attaining the highest aspirations of the human soul."

Today, leadership guru Mack R. Douglas echoes Roosevelt's words when he says: "Read biographies. Read constructive fantasies. Read books of faith and inspiration and, by all means, read the Bible."

I couldn't agree more. As for biographies and the Bible, no one can go wrong pulling books like these from the shelves and digging in.

I know suggesting the Bible is a controversial topic, but there's nothing wrong with a healthy discussion between two active minds. So I want to suggest that one of the first and most important books in anyone's collection should be the Bible. It doesn't matter which translation you choose. From 1611's King James Version to The Message (NavPress, 2002), they all tell the same story. And no matter what your religious background and beliefs, the Bible has a message for you.

The study of the Bible is a post-graduate course in the richest library of human experience.

—Herbert Hoover

I was intrigued when I read this recent statistic, attributed to Concordia University's Marie Wachlin: "Ninety-eight percent of the country's leading high-school English teachers believe biblical literacy gives students distinct educational advantages."

My writing partner in this book, Peggy Matthews Rose, agrees. Though she earned her college degree in English Literature, she told me it was only after she began to read and comprehend the Bible that what she had learned made complete sense. "The Bible is rich in symbolism and meaning," Peggy said. "Without this foundation, I believe any education is incomplete, at best. So many words I'd read, even by secular authors, only took on real meaning in the light of the Scriptures. It's funny, really, when you think about it, because certainly not all authors of classic literature were necessarily Christians. But truth resonates. We know it in our hearts, and it is confirmed in Scripture."

Wisdom is often associated with age, since we accrue it through time and experience. How often do you hear the phrase, "A wise old man once told me . . . "? I could be wrong, but I don't think I've ever seen a young person associated with wisdom, unless it was to point out its rare occurrence. But wisdom itself knows no age. The Bible is full of wisdom, which is why it is a timeless book, no matter how often we update the translations.

---

*A thorough knowledge of the Bible
is worth more than a college education.*

—Theodore Roosevelt

Historian Bill Federer tells of the time in 1921 when famed botanist George Washington Carver addressed the U.S. House Ways and Means Committee, detailing the product potential of the peanut. When asked by the chairman how he'd learned all the things he knew, Carver answered that he'd learned by reading "an old book."

"What book?" asked the chairman, and Carver answered, "The Bible."

Surprised, the chairman asked if the Bible actually talked about peanuts. "No, sir," Carver explained. "It tells about the God who made the peanut. I asked him to show me what to do with it, and he did."

One of my favorite contemporary dispensers of wisdom is the great Fred Smith. Even now he mentors Zig Ziglar, Bill Glass, and others. He has a much-visited website where he shares his views on leadership, business, faith, family, and so on. This true one-of-a-kind thinker offers as his fifth principle of decision making: "Make decisions according to Scriptural principles."

You'll never go wrong by following that advice, but you can't know what those principles are unless you read the Scriptures.

New Releases

Keeping current on trends of thought is critical in this rapidly changing landscape of life. That's not because we need to be "trendy." In fact, I'd argue against that waste of time. But we need to know what others are thinking, saying, and writing—and what impact those words and ideas might be having on those we care about, like our children. We need to know what people are shaping our culture, and usually they're the folks with books on the "new releases" table—whether they ought to be or not!

Read books on topics that don't pertain strictly to your business or industry. It's the best way to maintain a broad perspective.

—Bill Gates

You can keep up with new releases easily, on the front tables in your bookstores and through the book sections of your favorite periodicals. Books do more than just keep us current—they take us beneath the surface and help us discover the great treasures on the ocean floor.

Yes, there can be a lot of debris on that ocean floor, too, but that's where your well-honed, discerning eye comes into play. Keep your mind sharp by reading great thinkers, and it won't be long before you'll easily distinguish the pearls from the seaweed.

Bestsellers

True, bestsellers don't always qualify as great literature. It takes time—usually a lifetime—to arrive at that esteemed level. But books don't generally end up on bestseller lists unless they've got a message that's resonating with a lot of people. I check the *New York Times* book review on Sunday and the book section in the Thursday edition of *USA Today*. There are plenty of other resources for finding those lists. Even Amazon.com posts them. Check them often. Know what's out there, and read a bestseller now and then. Know what's influencing the folks around you. Or maybe there's a particular book you've discovered that happens to be a bestseller. Bring it up at the water cooler or the lunch table. Create your own disciples.

Choose Books That Uncover Truth

There must be something in books, things we can't imagine, to make a woman stay in a burning house; there must be something there. You don't stay for nothing.

—Fireman Guy Montag, following a house
book burning in Ray Bradbury's *Fahrenheit 451*

Have you ever felt frustrated that in this information age, "answers" come from every direction—but few of them agree? How can we know what's true and good and right? Truth vs. trash. If you look around, you'll see we are surrounded by both—every day! I once heard someone observe, "Trash gets dumped on us with no effort at all on our parts. We don't have to look for it. But truth needs to be sought out." Do you want truth? Look for it. Go below the surface. Mine the wisdom found in books.

If a book comes from the heart,
it will contrive to reach other hearts;
all art and authorcraft are of
small amount to that.

—Thomas Carlyle

Author Bruce Wilkinson cautions us, "Consider the words of the great American statesman Daniel Webster: 'If religious books are not widely circulated among the masses in this country, I do not know what is going to become of us as a nation. If truth be not diffused, error will be . . . if the power of the gospel is not felt throughout the length and breadth of the land, anarchy and misrule, degradation and misery, corruption and darkness will reign.' Twenty-six years after Webster made this statement, two men wrote a little booklet called *The Communist Manifesto.* When the dust had cleared, 60 million people were murdered and the course of history dramatically altered . . . all because of a book barely one hundred pages long."

Harriet Beecher Stowe understood the world in which slaves lived. Out of her own pain at the loss of a beloved child, she allowed her broken heart to feel what must have tormented so many mothers during that sad era in American history, as children were routinely ripped from their arms. Because Harriet Beecher Stowe cared enough to expose the cruel practice of slavery, a nation paid attention. Legend has it that in 1862, President Abraham Lincoln welcomed a visit from "the little lady who made this big war." *Uncle Tom's Cabin* opened people's eyes to a grave social injustice, a practice that had been indulged in for generations.

Books have an amazing power to uncover truth and provoke change.

Choose Books That Can Change Tomorrow

It's one thing to read books that impact your life, change your thinking, or give you a new heart—but what about ideas and information that influences the world you live in and the world you'll one day leave to others?

One columnist reminded me not long ago of how books can help us build bridges with people of other cultures, faiths, and backgrounds. We can find advice in books to help us cope with problems at work, illness in our families, relationships, religion, or even reasons for living. "Books," wrote Bill Ellis for *ASSIST News,* "will sharpen your mind. They will add comfort, truth, poise, freedom, confidence, and unbounded inspiration to your life." He is so right. And as books work *in* your life, they can work *through* your life, too.

Through books we can study the lessons of history and the hope—or warnings—that influence our future.

So while you may be drawn to the latest headlines or daily blogs, don't neglect the lessons of yesterday. No less a historian than David McCullough told *Newsweek* (May 23, 2005): "We are shaped by people we have never met. Yes, reading history will make you a better citizen and more appreciative of the law, and of freedom, and of how the economy works or doesn't work, but it is also an immense pleasure—the way art is, or music is, or poetry is. And it's never stale."

Armed with those lessons, we can apply them to all that cutting-edge stuff—the information and technology shaping our future. That's how it's supposed to work. If we neglect yesterday, we'll only have to go through the pain again.

The *What* Factor: So What Can I Do About It?

When you hear the phrase "for your information," what do you do? Do you pay attention, or do you tune out whatever follows? Some of us really don't want to be informed. Why? Maybe because we think we already know it all. Not true! In order for you to enjoy a more satisfying life-experience now, you must:

1. **Know what you're looking for—discover why you're here.** Look for books that help you understand the reasons for living. Many would have us believe that life is purposeless and void, but I don't believe that. I imagine you don't, either. If life were truly without meaning, why would any of this matter? You are here for a reason. Don't miss out on discovering what that reason is. Books are some of the best tools I know for self-discovery.

Life-transforming ideas have always come to me through books.

—Bell Hooks, professor of
English at City College, New York

---

2. **Know what you're here to do.** At some point along the way, each of us must answer the question, "What do I want to be when I grow up?" While some of us may still be asking that question well into our eighties, books help us refine that vision. Walt Disney observed, "Everyone has been remarkably influenced by a book, or books. In my case, it was a book on cartoon animation. I discovered it in the Kansas City Library at the time I was preparing to make motion-picture animation my life's work. The book told me all I needed to know as a beginner—all about the arts and the mechanics of making drawings that move on the theater screen. From the basic information, I could go on to develop my own way of storytelling."

Do you see what Walt discovered in that book? It became his university, his college training. That book gave him the foundation for his life's work. What it did *not* do was dictate the direction of his dream. Nowhere did it hint there was only one way to pursue his goal. It gave him the tools to become the unique visionary he was created to be.

Earlier we talked about reading books that challenge you to change your world. No one will argue that Walt Disney powerfully impacted the world we live in, during his lifetime and with his continuing legacy. How are you changing yours? What big dream do you have that a book can help you implement?

3. **Remember that you are connected to all those who've gone before you.** Who were they? What did they learn? How did they live? What were their dreams, hopes, and aspirations? The only way you can know them, now that they've gone on into eternity, is through books they may have left behind, or through history books written about them. Let the wisdom of ages past clothe your mind and dress your future decisions. Wisdom never goes out of style.

4. **Commit yourself to making a difference for someone else's future.** When I chose to become a husband, I joined my life with another's. Her future became intertwined with mine. Fatherhood extended that union. Then as I brought fourteen orphaned children into my home from four different countries, it was clear I was getting seriously involved in shaping more than a handful of future lives. Without the books that have become part of my life, I'd have been far less able to impact my kids for good. Books have been my counselors, my child-care gurus, my comforting shoulder during times of heartache.

Books can do all that for you and more. They can answer your questions, and they can inspire your dreams. Books can help you leave a legacy for enriching other lives.

5. **Know that you don't have all the answers.** Books help you

know what questions to ask. They guide your discovery as you travel the mysterious, sometimes painful, and often wonderful paths of life.

Start by making a list of things you've always wanted to know more about, or writers you've wanted to read, or current problems that perplex you. If you don't have any book titles in mind, take that list with you to a bookstore, library, or even your favorite online search engine (Amazon.com; barnesandnoble.com; booksdownload.org; Google.com; Gutenberg.org; powells.com—the possibilities are almost endless). You'll come out with a stack that's sure to get you started.

---

*To live fully your well-read life—
at any age—it is essential to take your selection
of books seriously. When you drift from book
to book, you are lulled into thinking that this lack
of focus is right and natural—but it's as wrong as
can be. Some serendipity in your reading is
delightful, but if you wanted to build a house,
would you wait for the materials
to assemble themselves?*

—Steve Leveen,
The Little Guide to Your Well-Read Life

Here are six tactics that may help you in making book selections:

1. **Look at the book jacket.** They say you shouldn't judge a book by its cover, but today's dust jackets are designed to help you do just that. By providing visual clues, endorse-

ments, synopses, and brief bios of the author, they offer valuable information that can help you decide if that book is worth a percentage of your paycheck, the Borders, Barnes & Noble, or Amazon gift certificate you got for Christmas—or your time.

2. **Find a favorite author.** Do you have a favorite author, or is there a series you're following? If you don't, you need to discover one or two. There are plenty of great writers out there, many of whom will strike a note with you. Some, like those popular Left Behind books written by my friends Jerry B. Jenkins and Bible scholar Tim LaHaye, can't come out fast enough for hungry serial readers. If you enjoy fiction, perhaps you're a fan of Stephen King, Tami Hoag, John Grisham, or another popular novelist. For nonfiction, my How to Be Like . . . series promises to introduce you to the lives and lessons of some of the world's great influencers. Anytime these authors release a new title, you have it on preorder. And sites like Amazon.com let you know in advance when a new title from your favorite author is about to launch. "Networking" in this way with your favorite authors is an excellent way to make sure you are reading regularly.

If you find you enjoy classic literature, your list has already been created. And what amazing, profound truths are there to be discovered in the timeless works of authors like Shakespeare, Milton, Dickens, Cervantes, and so many more. A reader could spend one hour every day just reading the great classics and never fully exhaust the list because, while there are no "new releases" in this category, new titles are being added on a regular basis. Those that stand the test of time, and resound in the hearts and minds of readers the world over, eventually join this coveted list.

---

*Temples fall, statues decay, mausoleums
perish, eloquent phrases declaimed are forgotten,
but good books are immortal.*

William T. Vernon

But what about between those series books or favorite authors? What do you do between publication dates? There are still plenty of great books out there. Why not look for a book in your professional field, or a field you'd like to explore, written by a leading authority? The right author can make your choice of what to read easier. Find someone with whom you connect, whose thoughts and ideas challenge you. That author can be contemporary or classic. What matters is that you read.

3. **Read book reviews.** If you're not sure where to start, check out the *New York Times Book Review* section, or another reputable publication. Whether your preferences are fiction or nonfiction, you'll find current works and information to help you make your choice.

4. **Browse the table of contents.** Next time you're in your favorite bookstore, spend some time looking through the books that appeal to you. A quick glance through the table of contents, a scan of the jacket blurbs, or skimming the first page or two can often tell you enough to know if a book is worth pursuing.

Today, you can bring public-domain titles right into your home through the Internet. Even now, you can read classic works on your computer screen. Personally, I prefer the feel of a book in my hands and the portability of carrying it with me wherever I go, but it's good to know great works of literature are being preserved and passed on in so many exciting ways.

With a menu that offers something for everyone, the future of reading is in good hands—as long as we all choose generously from that menu!

5. **Ask someone you know and respect.** Not sure where to begin building your personal library? Ask an expert— someone you admire, a leader or a reader whose opinion you value. Success sage Brian Tracy advises building a personal success library, beginning with people successful in your field of endeavor. "One of the marks of the professional, and professionalism is a state of mind, is that he has a library in his field," Tracy says. Think about it: the experts who write books have spent years learning their subject and possibly a few years writing the book. But you can learn the lessons that took a lifetime for them to learn in just a few focused hours of reading. Think of all the pain you can avoid!

6. **Visit my website.** I list books I have read and recommend to you. You'll find it at www.patwilliamsmotivate.com, and it's definitely about more than basketball. My dream is that, through this site, you'll find a book or two that lead to a book or two, that lead to a book or two . . . and on and on.

A library, to modify the famous metaphor of Socrates, should be the delivery room for the birth of ideas . . . a place where history comes to life.

—Norman Cousins, editor and writer

Above all other factors in deciding what to read is this: pursue your personal interests. Never pick up a book you're not interested in. My only hard and fast rule when it comes to read-ing is that you *must* find areas that interest you. We'll talk about that a little more a few chapters from now, when we take a field trip to the bookstore.

Before we leave this discussion of reading choices in our dust, I don't want to miss this "choice" advice from twentieth-century Canadian writer Robertson Davies: "A truly great book should be read in youth, again in maturity, and once more in old age, as a fine building should be seen by morning light, at noon, and by midnight." Truth has a way of impacting our lives in fresh and often profound ways from one season to the next. Words that passed before my eyes like so many pebbles yesterday can glint with the gold of longed-for answers today or tomorrow. Do you have a favorite book? Why not pull it off the shelf and give it another whirl soon? Anything worth reading once is usually worth reading again.

If reading has not played a major role in your life before now, I hope our discussion so far and the stack of books you've begun building has you convinced. But just in case you're still collecting them with someone else in mind, let's talk about *who* reads—with the goal of adding your name to this impressive list.

Read for Your Life Way No. 7:

Meet the *Who* Factor

11

Books Help You
Be More YOU

*O*kay, Pat, but only some people really need to read. Right?
Well, yes, that's right. And *you* are some people! Reading is one of the vital factors in helping you be you. Books have the power to help you define your values, determine your goals, and decide just who you are. In many ways, they are like the mirrors in which we see ourselves reflected. But rather than merely reflecting the image, books inform the image.

"The single greatest influence in your life is your own perspective," wrote Rick Warren. It's true. And that perspective is shaped and molded by a number of factors, not least among them the books you read. Let me tell you about two books that helped me discover, develop, and deliver my life perspective.

Books Reveal the *Real* YOU

By the early 1980s, my professional sports career was rocketing upward—but my speaking career was floundering. Requests were coming faster than Michael Jordan scored points—and I simply didn't know what to do. What kind of message could I deliver? As a lifetime reader, I did know where I'd find my answers—in books! And let me tell you, I did. *Expect to Win* (Word Books, 1982) and *Plan to Win* (Word Books, 1984), both by longtime NFL defensive end Bill Glass, were two clear, well-written motivational/success books whose material literally launched my speaking career. I'd never really known where to get material or how to craft a speech; these books told me how. They became my speaker's tutorials, helping me find and craft a lifetime message.

Glass, founder of the successful prison ministry Champions for Life, laid down clear principles of success that were right on the money. At that time in my life, as I was maturing and having success in sports, those books absolutely hit a button in my life and launched a message I have delivered literally thousands of times, I'm sure. By the way, I found his books as I find most books—on the front table of a bookstore.

Now here is another way books can impact your life and shape who you become: at the time I read those books, I didn't personally know Bill Glass. Today, I'm proud to call him a friend. If you don't read, there are a lot of great people you might never meet.

In addition to helping me frame my life message, those two books inspired a lifetime pursuit based on Bill Glass's materials and was foundational for a book I've written called *Who Wants to Be a Champion?* (Howard Publishing Company, August 2005). I dedicated it to Bill Glass.

Earlier, I told you about the amazing influence on my young heart and mind of a book called *Pop Warner's Book for Boys*. As I was writing this book, I came across an article by Michael Richman for *Investor's Business Daily*—all about Glenn "Pop" Warner. I'd say I couldn't believe it, but "coincidences" like this one seem to accompany nearly every book I've written. Richman says Warner was a man who didn't want to forget anything, so he always carried around a pencil and scrap paper in order to write down anything interesting he saw or heard.

Now that may not seem like a crucial observation to you, but it turns out I do almost that very thing! Have all my life. I'm known for the notes I take everywhere I go, the quotes, facts, and ideas I collect. It's interesting to consider the subliminal effect ol' Pop Warner himself may have had on me.

Richman also points out Pop Warner's insistence on good sportsmanship, a fact I referred to earlier. "If his team lost, he wouldn't allow grumbling. His players always had to compliment the other team when it won." About teamwork, Richman notes, Pop Warner instructed, "Don't be a grandstand player . . . it's the team that counts, and the grandstander soon finds that nobody is willing to block for him. The way to get good blocking is to block for the other fellow. To become a great athlete, you must earn the benefit of teamwork." Imagine that—old Pop was teaching servant leadership more than fifty years ago. Could it be that authors writing and speaking on this topic today were influenced by Pop Warner, way back when they were kids? It's a possibility.

Everything you want to do in life, reading can help you accomplish it. There are few things better at nourishing the mind than reading.

—Paul Allen,
cofounder of Microsoft

Today, of course, I know that Pop was raising the bar for us kids. He knew the truth—he'd been in collegiate athletics all his life. But he also knew that with the right adult influences, we could soar to unimagined heights.

Books by men like Pop Warner and Bill Glass illustrate the old saying, "No one cares how much you know until they know how much you care." These are books written by men who were passionate about kids, devoted to developing young lives, setting them on the right track, or correcting those who had taken a wrong turn.

When I look at those three books still in my library—books I first read many, many years ago—it's clear they powerfully influenced the man I have become.

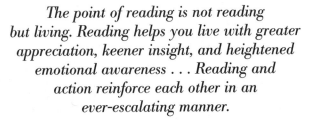

The point of reading is not reading but living. Reading helps you live with greater appreciation, keener insight, and heightened emotional awareness . . . Reading and action reinforce each other in an ever-escalating manner.

—Steve Leveen, author

Have you ever heard the phrase, "There's nothing new under the sun"? Trying to find our way in life, that special niche in which we fit, can be discouraging until we realize our uniqueness. Our experiences may not be new, but how they influence us is. After all, there's never been another *you* before! And because of that fact, the way you use the experiences of your life to influence others makes something new happen for them. Through books, we discover how others handled problems or solved dilemmas; how they shouldered pain, trouble, and sorrow; how they overcame seemingly impossible obstacles. Without books, even the most brilliant, uniquely personal perspective can have limited influence on the life of another.

In 1760, Methodist founder John Wesley advised fellow preacher John Trembeth on how to avoid the rut of mediocrity. Wesley observed: "What has exceedingly hurt you in time past, nay, and I fear to this day, is want of reading . . . Hence your talent in preaching does not increase . . . Reading only can supply this, with meditation and daily prayer. You wrong yourself greatly by omitting this . . . Fix some part of every day for private exercises."

Books expand our personal horizons.

In talking about her first role as a radio broadcaster, Oprah Winfrey said, "I can't imagine where I'd be or who I'd be had reading not been such a fundamental tool in my life. After years of reading everything I could get my hands on, reciting poetry to whoever would listen, someone was going to pay me to do what I loved—read out loud."

In Denzel Washington's book *A Hand to Guide Me* (Meredith Books, 2006), I found the story of former CNN anchor Bernard Shaw's meeting with journalism idol Walter Cronkite. Shaw, a young military officer at the time, asked the great newsman's advice about working toward his career goals once his stint of duty was over and he'd gone back to school. Cronkite noted that a reporter needed to know a little bit about everything, and that nothing would give him a better sense of all there is in life than to "read, read, read." Shaw added that he now shares that advice with every young person he can.

Whoever you want to become in life, books can help you get there. Someone, somewhere, has done what you want to do before you. Learn from their mistakes; profit from their losses. Value their wisdom. Are you looking for a mentor? Books can fill that role in so many ways.

I believe that all of us are given gifts—skills and talents to use while we are here on Earth. My gifts involve team building, and over the years, books have helped me strengthen those abilities. My career in professional sports has benefited from books; my development as a human being has been altered and strengthened by books; my understanding of life and its true meaning has been blessed and expanded by books.

C. S. Lewis observed, "The more we let God take us over, the more truly ourselves we become—because he made us. He invented all the different people that you and I were intended to be." One of the ways I believe God "takes us over" is through the interchange of thoughts and ideas with other members of his creation—and that includes everyone ever born. Books are the best way I've found to gather those ideas. Books offer a permanent record. Unlike conversations or even great lectures, books are like the searchable thoughts of the author. Books are one of God's tools for helping you and me become all we're meant to be. I'd hate to arrive in eternity and find out I'd missed something important—wouldn't you?

Seek the lofty, by reading,
hearing, and seeing great work,
at some moment, every day.

—Thornton Wilder, playwright

Books Introduce You to Fascinating People

One of my favorite book categories is biographies. I love learning about other people whose lives have changed the world. In fact, I've *written* several. Biographies can help us meet people we would never have the opportunity to know any other way, and they can teach us lessons from those lives we can apply to our own. They may be about great figures from history, or heroes who live in our own hometown. My own How to Be Like . . . series has spanned the gamut from Jesus, to Walt Disney, to Rich DeVos, to Michael Jordan, to women of influence, to Jackie Robinson, to John Wooden. All these people have made a difference in my life. Who do you want to learn from?

Bruce Wilkinson, founder of Walk Through the Bible and author of *Prayer of Jabez*, notes, "Reading is the lifeline of civilization. It was reading David Brainerd's biography that moved William Carey to found a mission board and send scores of missionaries into India with the gospel. It was reading George MacDonald and G. K. Chesterton that forced C. S. Lewis's agnostic mind to come to grips with the God of the universe."

Motivational speaker and author Hal Urban recalls the rich lessons gained from reading biographies of famous Americans. "Nothing," he said, "helps us understand the meaning of success better than reading about people who made the most of their lives" (*Life's Greatest Lessons: 20 Things That Matter,* Fireside, 2002).

Bruce Barton, twentieth-century ad-agency executive, congressman, and author, once addressed a woman who asked him to recommend a list of books for her son. "Start him with a *Life of Lincoln*; then a *Life of Washington*; then a *Life of Cromwell*; and Franklin's autobiography. When he has read these, I will recommend some more." Barton, who was known for his ability to understand the consumer viewpoint, kept a library of more than 1,000 volumes, mostly biographies or books of history.

---

*There is perhaps nothing more interesting
to many minds than a good biography; it has all
the charm of fiction with all the satisfaction
of being real. I say real rather than true, because
no man in a biography or autobiography
can write the exact truth.*

—William Lyon Phelps, former professor of English at Yale University

---

Reading about great men and women of history—both past and present—shapes our thoughts, our values, and even our actions. Whether we are contemporaries or not, whether we ever meet personally, whether or not we come to know one another in this lifetime, we are all connected by the fact of having lived on this Earth. We owe it to ourselves and to our posterity to get to know each other, those who share the oxygen with us now and those who've breathed it in times past. Books offer a great avenue for making those connections.

One other thing about biographies: learning about people we admire influences our character, as well. As guru Fred Smith says, "Study the biographies of great men and you soon realize that the great are grateful."

Get to Know Writers

I realized that a man was behind each one of the books. A man had to think them up. A man had to take a long time to put them down on paper . . . It took some man a lifetime maybe to put some of his thoughts down . . .

–Fireman Guy Montag, in *Fahrenheit 451*

Reading opens our minds to different perspectives, cultures, eras, and information we just can't get any other way. That's what Bradbury's fictitious fireman, Guy Montag, discovered. Sure, we can learn a lot from TV shows and movies, but in books we are challenged to think and reflect as we actively interact with the mind of another human being. That person—the author—may be as close as your family or hometown, or as far away as a thousand years or a million miles.

You and I are exchanging thoughts, ideas, and opinions right here in these pages. I may not be able to read or hear what you're thinking, but my words are influencing you, creating community between us. Fred Smith, one of my favorite leadership mentors, puts it this way, "Do you live in a neighborhood of truly interesting people, even great ones? If not, would you like to? You can when you surround yourself with the books these people have written—and those written about them."

Through our thoughts and ideas, you and I are also connecting right now. Words and the way we use them shape our minds. So reading offers mind stretching, mental aerobics, and strength training all in one. Because you are reading this book, my friend, you and I are connected for all eternity—through the transcending power of words and the ideas they form. Isn't that an awesome truth? I think it is.

"Would you like to talk with Einstein?" asks Smith. "Then open a book of his essays. Had you rather listen to Emerson? He is in the library at your convenience." Now that is a provocative thought, indeed. Consider how many people you would love to spend time with—people you admire, people you would love to get to know personally. The problem is, they are untouchable. Books make people touchable, readable, knowable.

Through books, you not only have the opportunity to meet writers, but sometimes a book can become a vehicle for you to meet its main character—for real. Like the time I spotted a book that wouldn't let go of me until I bought it. *Veeck as in Wreck* was its title. I was a young ballplayer in those days, just twenty-two years of age. But oh, I knew the name Veeck. Who didn't? Since the 1940s, Bill Veeck had owned a string of ball clubs, like the Cleveland Indians, the St. Louis Browns, and the Chicago White Sox. His antics for bringing in crowds were notoriously funny and outrageous. He was also my hero.

I had just signed a contract with the Phillies organization as a catcher. They sent me to Miami in the Florida State League, and that's where I debuted in June 1962. One day that season, I ended up in Burdine's department store in downtown Miami, where I wandered through the book section. There was that book. It had just come out. I was immediately riveted by the picture on the dust jacket and that title: *Veeck as in Wreck,* the memoirs of this great promoter and flamboyant owner of major-league teams. Forty-three years later, that book is still in print. Astonishingly, it continues to show up in sports sections of bookstores. In it, Bill talked about his career and his unique approach to marketing sports, to selling the product. And it was written in such a wonderfully direct and amusing way. I was deeply impacted.

Reading gives delight, information, stimulation, and ability. The wise crave it, the superficial discourage it, and the stupid neglect it.

—Haddon Robinson, communicator

Amazingly enough, in the first chapter, mention was made of a man named Bill Durney, who just happened to be the general manager of our minor-league team in Miami at that time. Durney had been an associate of Bill Veeck's in St. Louis—a close friend! When that season ended, I said to Bill Durney, "More than anything in the world, I would like to meet Bill Veeck." At that time, Veeck was living in retirement in Easton, Maryland, about two hours from my home in Wilmington, Delaware. Through Bill Durney's friendship, I was able to go to Bill Veeck's estate in September of that year. Like a starstruck kid, I spent five hours with him—five hours that developed into a twenty-five-year friendship and mentorship. And it all started with that book— *Veeck as in Wreck.*

I still have that book, by the way. I couldn't tell you where *Pop Warner's Book for Boys* is, but I know exactly where *Veeck as in Wreck* is. I looked at the price tag the other day: $3.95—for a 400-page-plus hardcover book! And, by the way, Bill Veeck's signature was in the front of the book when I bought it.

My point is, you never know who you'll meet when you pick up a book. You may just spend a few hours in another person's mind, or you may make a friend for life—someone who'll literally change your life. But if you never pick up the book, you could be missing the adventure of a lifetime.

Reading was my escape and my comfort,
my consolation, my stimulant of choice:
reading for the pure pleasure of it,
for the beautiful stillness that surrounds you
when you hear an author's words
reverberating in your head.

—Paul Austere, author

A beautiful friendship started with that book. For the next twenty-five years, Bill Veeck was a friend, a mentor, a major influence in my life. In retrospect, I'm probably the way I am today largely because in 1969, after one year with the Philadelphia 76ers, Bill Veeck recommended me to the ownership of the Chicago Bulls to be their general manager. That led to an interview, which led to the job. And at age twenty-nine, I became one of the youngest GMs in sports history, as general manager of the Chicago Bulls. Bill Veeck was the reason, and it all started from reading his book seven years prior to that. So one never knows about the impact of a book.

Not long ago, it was my pleasure to share this story with Jack Canfield and Gay Hendricks for their examination of life-changing books, *You've GOT to Read This Book!* (HarperCollins, 2006). What a joy to be featured with fifty-four of my contemporaries in this discussion of books that have literally changed our life trajectories.

My friends, I cannot encourage you enough to look for all the possible connections in your life available to you through books.

The Greek poet Pindar once said, "Words have a longer life than deeds." There is no doubt about that fact. Some deeds may live on after you do, but even if you're an architect who builds great buildings or a visionary who builds great companies, your legacy is likely to be little more than a nameplate fifty years after you're gone. People—their thoughts, their words, their essence—live on through books.

Speaking of people, there are more than a few movers and shakers throughout history whose lives were largely powered by the books they read. Let me introduce you to a few of them.

12

Meet a Few People Who Care About Reading

When I read about great people—people I admire or whose lives inspire me—and find out their dreams were driven by books they read, it affirms me. It verifies my heartfelt belief that reading matters, that books make a lasting difference. So who cares about reading? Who are some of these history-makers who led book-powered lives?

This fact might surprise you, given the often-prevailing attitude toward politicians, but many of our U.S. presidents have placed enormous stock in reading—including current officeholder George W. Bush. I've mentioned his reading habits elsewhere in this book. He's a voracious reader.

And he's in good company. Throughout history, many of our greatest leaders led lives shaped, in large part, by books. Let's meet a few of them.

George Washington

America's first George W., George Washington, was also an avid reader. According to biographer Edward G. Lengel, "Reading . . . provided him a lifetime of pleasure and learning that gradually compensated for his early deficiencies in spelling and grammar . . . An enthusiastic book collector, he also opened and read most of what he purchased." Washington is known to have been partial to books on agriculture, natural history, and military history and theory. Clearly, he applied much of what he read.

Longtime Yankees broadcaster Mel Allen was an avid reader. Devoured everything from biographies about famous figures like Franklin Delano Roosevelt and Winston Churchill to mystery novels to book-of-the-month selections.

–Stephen Borelli, author

James Madison

All I've learned about America's Founding Fathers tells me they all believed in the power of reading. Lynne Cheney writes of James Madison:

> Rightly known as the father of our Constitution, he was the prime mover behind that magnificent document and known as well as the primary author of the Bill of Rights.
>
> The knowledge that enabled these achievements came in large part from reading, an occupation to which Madison dedicated himself from his youngest years. Even as a boy, he knew the power of the printed word to enlarge experience. He saw how books could teach

about times and places that one could otherwise never know.

During his college years . . . Madison encountered more books than he had ever seen before and well-trained minds to test himself against . . . As early as 1783, Madison began an intensive course of reading to assess the alternatives [to the Articles of Confederation]. He implored his friend Thomas Jefferson, then in Paris, to send him books.

In spite of the fact that he never traveled far from where he was born, Cheney points out, Madison profoundly influenced the shaping of American thought. "And from within it," she writes, "using books as his lever, he managed to move the world."

Benjamin Franklin

Though never a U.S. president, Ben Franklin is without doubt one of our greatest statesmen, and called by editor Blaine McCormick, "America's Original Entrepreneur." In Franklin's autobiography, adapted by McCormick, Franklin wrote: "Since my childhood I've loved reading, and every cent that came my way I used to purchase books." Franklin's love of books and readings was evident to his father, who set him to work as a printer, apprenticing to his older brother, James, when he was just twelve years old. One wealthy customer, who also noted young Franklin's passion, invited him to read any of the books in his extensive library. These volumes exposed Ben's young mind to a variety of writing styles and thoughts, all of which eventually wove themselves into the person this great statesman later became. Through books, Franklin honed his writing skills, continually challenging himself to become better at what he was already good at.

January 17, 2006, marked the 300th anniversary of Ben Franklin's birth. What a rich legacy he left, through his many inventions—including the bifocals for which I am grateful today—his bold stance for liberty, his powerful entrepreneurial spirit and sense of persistence, and so much more.

Perhaps above all, Franklin was a prolific author and a man who lived a singularly remarkable life. As a printer who worked with movable type, Franklin had rich opportunities to work with words. It's no wonder he learned to use them so well. Franklin stirred hearts and minds to action with his pioneering newspaper, the *Pennsylvania Gazette*. As a diplomat, he defined America, and is largely regarded today as the First American. Books framed and formed this singular life.

Abraham Lincoln

Not only was he one of history's greatest leaders, Abraham Lincoln was one of history's most devoted readers. Doris Kearns Goodwin writes of Lincoln, "Books became his academy, his college. The printed word united his mind with the great minds of generations past. Relatives and neighbors recalled that he scoured the countryside for books and read every volume 'he could lay his hands on.' At a time when ownership of books remained 'a luxury for those Americans living outside the purview of the middle class,' gaining access to reading material proved difficult. When Lincoln obtained copies of the King James Bible, John Bunyan's *Pilgrim's Progress*, Aesop's *Fables*, and William Scott's *Lessons in Elocution*, he could not contain his excitement. Holding *Pilgrim's Progress* in his hands, 'his eyes sparkled, and that day he could not eat, and that night he could not sleep.'"

Lincoln committed much of what he read to memory, convinced that people throughout history could not possibly have understood the capacity of their minds to improve before the printing press was invented, making reading possible for all mankind. I don't know about you, but that thought arrests my attention. To think there was a time when people would not have had the capability to expand their minds—and that we now have books freely available for the expanding. How can we ignore the power of a book? That Lincoln committed so much to memory speaks to the notion he knew that as books had so relatively recently appeared on the historical scene, they could be taken away.

While U.S. presidents read about other presidents for guidance and solace, partly why presidents read is the reason that we all read: to relax, to replenish our energy, and to go into another era, another time.

—Doris Kearns Goodwin,
presidential historian

"Everywhere he went, Lincoln carried a book with him," Kearns Goodwin wrote. "He thumbed through page after page while his horse rested at the end of a long row of planting. Whenever he could escape work, he would lie with his head against a tree and read . . . Reading the Bible and Shakespeare over and over implanted rhythms and poetry that would come to fruition in those works of his maturity that made Abraham Lincoln our only poet-president."

He once borrowed a volume called *Life of George Washington*, by Parson Weems, from a neighbor who lived sixteen miles away. The book was so badly damaged during a rainstorm, Lincoln vowed to work and repay the price of the book. He did two full days of labor pulling corn. Abraham Lincoln knew the value of words.

Lincoln also knew the loneliness of being a reader in a world of nonreaders. Today we readers exult in the joy of sharing our latest word treasures with one another, but Lincoln was a world apart from those who lived in his little farming community. There were few with whom he could share the thoughts and feelings that books stirred within him. As he grew, what he lacked in formal education, he made up for through diligent, determined reading.

The where, when, and how of reading mattered not to Abraham Lincoln, who said, "The books, and your capacity for understanding them, are just the same in all places . . . Always bear in mind that your own resolution to succeed, is more important than any other thing."

In love as in life, Lincoln found himself attracted to intelligent, well-read women. Mary Todd, writes Kearns Goodwin, "shared Lincoln's love for discussing books and poetry."

Learn the lesson of Lincoln's life: books shape your decisions, your thoughts, and your actions. Who wouldn't love to have this man's mastery of oratory?

Harry S. Truman

Biographer David McCullough tells this story of Harry Truman: "In the evenings he would turn to his books and become wholly immersed. 'You could talk to him if he were reading, and you wouldn't get an answer.' Indeed, Margaret [Truman] could not recall her father sitting down quietly at home without a book in his hand."

Further, McCullough notes, "President Truman was a prodigious reader, and each night he would carry home a portfolio, often six or eight inches thick. The next morning he would have gone through all that material and taken such action as was needed."

I never recall being bored—not once—
because we had a houseful of books.

—Harry S. Truman

As a youngster, McCullough writes, Truman and a pal once vowed to read every volume housed in their high-school library, encyclopedias included. "Reading history, to me, was far more than a romantic adventure," Truman once said. "It was solid instruction and wise teaching which I somehow felt that I wanted and needed." When asked once what her father's idea of heaven would be, daughter Margaret quickly responded, "Oh, to have a good comfortable chair, a good reading lamp, and lots of books around that he wanted to read" (*Truman*, Simon & Schuster, 1992).

I think old Harry was on to something.

Winston Churchill

Winston Churchill, the late British prime minister and one of the greatest world leaders of all time, had difficulty navigating school. Do you know anyone like that? While strides are continually being made, there will always be students for whom traditional classroom structure fails.

Here's what Churchill did about it. "Churchill recognized that his formal education had been inadequate for a would-be politician," writes biographer Steven F. Hayward.

"So I resolved to read history, philosophy, economics, and things like that," admitted Churchill. "It was a curious education."

Because his reading was largely self-guided, Churchill read unhampered by "experts" to advise his choices. While serving military duty in India, "Churchill read as much as five hours a day, often 'three or four books at a time to avoid tedium.'" Churchill's reading list included such "bestsellers" as Gibbon's *Decline and Fall of the Roman Empire*, the history volumes of Thomas McCauley, Plato, Aristotle, and Charles Darwin—to name a handful. When it came to reading, Churchill was no slouch. He seemed to understand this principle: great vision comes from great ideas, and great ideas are often found in books.

Ronald Reagan had the smarts . . .
He craved reading, a love that he got from
his mother . . . Reagan once told me, . . .
"Mike, Nelle told me that if you learn to
love reading you will never be alone."

—Michael Deaver, Reagan campaign advisor

George S. Patton

Would you believe that George S. Patton, one of the greatest leaders in U.S. military history, suffered from dyslexia? They didn't call it that back when he was a boy, but nonetheless, he displayed all the classic symptoms. He had tremendous difficulty recognizing and comprehending written words. Today, we've given that problem a name, and we've discovered ways to treat it, but back in Patton's day, it was simply known as being "slow." Children like Patton were set back in school and ridiculed by their peers.

To what do we owe Patton's victory over this dark difficulty? Biographer Alan Axelrod attributes it to Patton's parents, who refused to look the other way, and to a personal drive to be not simply normal, but more than normal. By the time he emerged from the world of private tutors to enroll in a private boys' school at the age of eleven, Patton had become a history buff. He avidly read the accounts of great captains of the past—Scipio Africanus, Hannibal, Caesar, Joan of Arc, Napoleon Bonaparte, Robert E. Lee, and Stonewall Jackson.

"Those who knew Patton as an adult," Axelrod writes, "could not help but observe that he was an avid reader . . . The historical figures of whom he read were superimposed upon his own experience. Lifelong, he devoured libraries of history, especially the history of ancient conquest, general military history, and the memoirs of celebrated generals."

Books fueled this young man's dreams. They gave him heroes and role models and hope. Who knows how much America owes to those writers throughout the ages who have taken time to write about great men and women like George S. Patton? It is their lives—most often lives that have overcome tremendous obstacles—that become the inspiration, the spark that ignites greatness in others.

Billy Graham

Billy Graham is one of the most influential figures of the twentieth century and beyond. What's the secret of his significance? One key factor, certainly, is his keen mind, fed by a heart that's continually hungry to learn. A lifelong passion for personal growth has helped make Billy Graham a man with much to offer a hurting world. This fervor has ignited his message and set hundreds of thousands of hearts afire over the years.

One life in particular that has been forever impacted by the influence of Billy Graham is that of his daughter, Ruth. In her book *A Legacy of Faith: Things I Learned from My Father*, Ruth Graham tells us, "Now in his late eighties, my father spends hours each day reading, usually propped up in his bed, which is framed on each side by bookcases—in fact, the room's paneled walls are lined with bookcases . . . My father doesn't read with a lot of props like notebooks and highlighters. He just takes notes, usually with felt-tip pens, in the book or Bible he happens to be reading. I have a Bible that contains his handwritten sermon notes in the margins and an outline inside the front cover . . ."

Though he's largely retired from speaking, Graham's relentless drive keeps him going. It hones his mind to stay active, sharp, and alive. "Because he loves to read, I usually give my father books for

Christmas," Ruth Graham continues. "One year I gave him a biography of George Washington that he referenced several times during dinner conversation. Following the September 11th attacks, he did extensive reading on Islam and its history, often raising the subject for discussion when I visited him."

Without doubt, it's this love of books and reading that has given him an edge in delivering life-changing messages over his long career. Ruth Graham affirms this when she writes, "If there is an area in which my father has consistently done his best, it is in preparation for preaching . . . He understands that the grace of God needs a prepared mind on which to operate.

"My father read all that he could on relevant subjects—the works of people like John Stott, James Montgomery Boice, and other Bible scholars and theologians."

The power of preparation, as Graham's career testifies, is not necessarily about reading to create the perfect four-point message. "Ruth [Graham's wife and Ruth Graham's mother] . . . believed, as I did," Graham said, "that God would give me the message and bring to remembrance in my preaching the things I had studied. This was always the most effective preaching . . . Hence, I picked each sermon topic carefully, read myself full, wrote myself empty, and read myself full again on that subject."

Wouldn't you love to have a life that makes the kind of difference Billy Graham's has? Books, as Billy testifies, are the key to that influence.

In a recent article, the eighty-seven-year-young evangelist confessed, "The greatest regret I have is that I didn't study more and read more. I regret it because now I feel at times I am empty of what I would like to have been." Does that comment from this amazing man stun you? It certainly does me. He understands the difference books can make in who we become. Don't miss that!

James A. Garfield

If that name doesn't immediately ring a bell, it's because this twentieth president of the United States held office for just one hundred and twenty days before an assassin's bullet ended his career—and his life. Garfield was a man who lived his dash well, accomplishing several great things during his brief time in office as a result. In an article for *Investor's Business Daily* (May 26, 2006), Curt Schleier describes a man with a voracious hunger to learn and a passion to help his fellow man—desires fed largely by reading. Before composing his inaugural address, Schleier wrote, "He read the inaugural addresses of all of his predecessors, evaluating what he felt they did right—and wrong."

Garfield understood that reading is our key to understanding the past and preparing for the future. He knew that without the records of his predecessors, without the tracks they had laid for his journey, his presidency would be shallow at best.

Dare to be like James A. Garfield, and all the other great people we've spent time with in this chapter.

In addition to these great historical figures, many other influential people have expressed gratitude for the ability to read . . . people like columnist William Raspberry, born in 1935 to a poor but loving black family in Mississippi, who thanked his parents for instilling in him a desire to read. That desire led to a forty-year career of persuading American thought through Raspberry's own way with words.

Tech leaders like Yang Yuanging, chairman of Chinese PC maker Lenovo, have had their thinking influenced by books. In a *USA Today* article, Yuanging listed the books *Built to Last* by Jim Collins and Jerry I. Porras, and *The World Is Flat* by Thomas L. Friedman, as valuable resources for solid principles of the past and insight into future trends. I'd say he should know, wouldn't you?

Note to Bookstore Owners:
Tap into the Power of Personality

What do you do when you've found something that excites you? If you're like me, you rush to tell someone else. You're hoping they'll get excited, too. Books offer many opportunities like that. When I read a great book on sports, I know many people in my profession who'll also enjoy the read. I can hardly wait to recommend it. Books on history, biographies that charge my batteries, leadership books that make their points in fresh new ways—those all go on the reading list on my website.

We'll talk more about bookstores later on, but right now, while we're talking about the "who" factor, I want to address bookstore owners. Do you know who works for you? Have you got any idea what readers and potential leaders you have on your own payroll?

Not long ago, I read a piece in *Publishers Weekly* that got my attention. Columnist Seth Godin addressed the contemporary bookstore experience from the customer-service perspective.

Tell me, have you ever walked into a bookstore intent on buying one book, and come out with several more, just because a sales associate recommended them? If you have, I'm guessing it wasn't last week. Or last year. Too many stores today rely on flashy displays, bestseller lists, and merchandising techniques to sell books, and too little on the personal side. "Handsold" books, says Godin, are giving way to self-sold books. And I say it's a shame—not simply because of the obvious boost to your bottom line, owners, but because of the crying need for *positive* interaction between sales personnel and buyers. I'm sure it betrays my age, but I recall when those folks behind the counters, the smiling faces stocking the shelves, were the ones we went to with questions, the experts we asked for advice. We expected them to be knowledgeable—and they did not disappoint us.

When you sell a man a book, you don't sell him twelve ounces of paper and ink and glue—you sell him a whole new life.

—Christopher Morley, early twentieth-century writer and editor

No more. In all too many cases, a question today is met with a shrug, an excuse, or a cold, uninformed reply—and that's *if* we can even find someone to ask! One of the charms unique to the old, dusty bookstores was the passion of the bookseller. We can do without the dust, but we do not have to give up the passion. Encourage your sales associates to read and recommend their favorite books. You'll be surprised what it does for your sales, your frontline enthusiasm, and your customer loyalty, as well. Here's Godin's advice: "If I ran a retail store, I'd get rid of a third of the books and rearrange the rest into a circle of discovery. I'd find clerks who were excited to be there and reward them for telling stories about the work that's there to be discovered. I'd hire a dozen summer interns at a time and let them get good at telling stories . . . I'd remember every customer.

"I'm not talking about going through the motions—I'm talking about reinventing the bookstore, turning it into a destination where customers fulfill desires they might not even have known they had before they walked through the door."

I'm not a retailer, I'm a customer . . . but I believe Godin is right on the money.

Clearly books have cared for and fed many great minds. Shouldn't they nourish yours? While we're on the subject, I'll bet I can surprise you with a few others I know who are passionate about reading.

*"I'm already reading twenty-five
other books, so why am I buying this one?"
I asked a friend. "Do you think this is a disease?"
"Yes," interjected the cashier.
"But it's a good disease to have."*

—Joe Queenan, *New York Times
Book Review* essay, August 8, 2006

13

Meet a Few
Sports Authorities

I've spent all of my adult life in the world of professional sports, and I'm fully aware that there is little similarity between the image of Washington Irving's bookish Ichabod Crane and your average all-American jock. Yet I've discovered, to my great delight, that books matter to many of my colleagues. What a thrill that so many successful sports figures credit their achievement to books.

Jerry West, president of the Memphis Grizzlies and former Los Angeles Lakers owner, coach, and player, told me, "Reading is important to me and a big part of my life. I want to keep learning and growing, so I read everything I can get my hands on in the areas of inspiration, self-help, and leadership. I can't get enough of these kinds of books." Folks, you can't argue with Jerry's success.

"Education—whether from a book or from experience—is the single most important key to success," said Arte Moreno, successful businessman and owner of the Los Angeles Angels of Anaheim. "I'm one of those people who reads self-help books all the time. Others read fiction, and I read how I can sell four widgets instead of three."

Phil Jackson, popular coach of the Los Angeles Lakers, told me, "I always take a stack of books with me on our road trips, and I encourage the players to do the same thing. Reading provides a wonderful escape from the drudgery of trains, planes, and buses we are riding. Books are a wonderful companion on a lonely night in a hotel room in a strange city."

Thank you, Phil, and to all the others like you who are setting the example for our players and their fans. What a great service you are doing by encouraging books as a healthy road-trip alternative.

If we have any hope of raising the bar for our young people, of showing them there are better ways to live than sliding into the moral and intellectual cesspool that tugs at them from every side, we've got to turn their eyes and minds away from the junk that's being produced today. Books provide far better tools for shaping young minds than reality TV shows or sitcoms that portray people hopping into bed with anything that breathes.

As role models go, there is no one on a higher plane in the eyes of most youngsters than champion athletes. Sadly, we hear all too often of the ones who misuse their celebrity status, men and women who make disastrous lifestyle choices simply because they can. A few moments of thoughtless "fun" whiplashes their lives off the courts and into endless weeks of courtroom drama, and they quickly discover the price for that temporary pleasure was a lot higher than they realized.

The good news is, those headline honchos are not the norm. Most professional athletes are far more dedicated to excellence in their chosen careers than shenanigans off the court or ball field. I know this to be true; I've been hanging with them for more than forty years. What's more—and this may surprise you, given the stereotypes—a great many of them are serious, dedicated readers. These champions know that fitness is more than just a physical necessity—without fit minds, our bodies are pretty much worthless.

⚜

Sports were important to him, to be sure,
but nothing could take the place of his cherished
collection of books. [Woody] Hayes developed
a discipline with books early on, so much so
in fact that he pursued education with
a hunger that usually only the best
and brightest pupils exhibit.

—Steve Greenberg,
biographer

Meet a Few Surprising Examples

I'm encouraged to know there are many other readers out there in the world of sports. NBA star Steve Nash is known for reading such works as the autobiography of Che Guevara, the *Communist Manifesto*, and *The Brothers Karamazov*. Good thing his touch with the basketball is lighter than his choice of reading material!

It's true that life for an athlete leaves little time for extra activities. But people like my friend Otis Smith, general manager for the Orlando Magic, give me great hope. "I am crazy about reading," Smith recently told *MAGIC Magazine*. "I probably go through eight to ten books a month, but I'd like to read another eight to ten a month if I could."

What an exemplary goal, both for Smith personally and for those influenced by his leadership. What we get from books lasts far longer than the momentary glow of a winning basketball score. What makes Smith's reading habit even greater, though, is his motivation for doing it. "I read because I'm trying to make myself better," he said, "so I can make other people better."

To prove he's a man of his word, at the end of last season, Smith gave each player on the Magic team a book called *Season of Life*, about teamwork, trust, and turning boys into men. "My job is to make them better," Smith explained. And that is true leadership.

---

*If you read, you submit your thoughts
to others' ideas and points of view. It gives you
a different perspective to life and makes you think.
When you read you are provided with
a whole series of thrills and chills.*

—Phil Jackson,
Los Angeles Lakers coach

Yankees star Alex Rodriguez, who signed with the Mariners just out of high school instead of going on to college, has found there are ways to make up for missing out on a formal education. "I love to read," Rodriguez told me. "I decided at age eighteen I wanted to learn, and reading is the best way to do that. I've got fourteen books or so going at the same time. I've always got a big stack of them going, and if I get bored with one, I move on to another one. I like to read about business and success because I'm always looking for an edge to improve myself."

Early life influences matter for all of us, no matter what we eventually become in life. When kids are surrounded by reading adults, they're likely to see reading as a lifelong value. Ray Allen, star player for the Seattle SuperSonics, told me not long ago, "As a child, I noticed that most of the people I looked up to and respected all read. I figured out reading would be a way for me to learn definitions of words and get smarter."

"I love to read," confessed the Magic's Grant Hill. "I'm an avid reader."

Charlotte Bobcats rookie star Adam Morrison is living evidence that sports professionals are often well read and have varied interests, even off the court. "I enjoy reading because it gives me a wide range of other people's views," Morrison told me. "I particularly like reading books on the political field. That's my main interest."

Athletes in all areas of excellence are big readers.

Olympic runner Gail Devers told me she reads a 350-page book every day!

Geno Auriemma, the highly successful coach of the University of Connecticut's women's basketball team, has said, "If anyone ever asked me the one thing that stands out in my life, it would be the ability to read and write."

Writer Austin Murphy said of Michigan Wolverine's coach Lloyd Carr (University of Michigan), "A voracious reader, he is deft at dropping quotations from such disparate figures as Thomas Jefferson, Rudyard Kipling, and George Patton. He frequently shares with his players passages from books he admires" (*Sports Illustrated*, November 20, 2006).

The late great coach John McKay, known as the "winningest" coach in USC Trojan football history, frequently boasted, "I try to read a book a day."

Legendary Ohio State football coach Woody Hayes grew up in a reading home. In his examination, *Buckeye Madness: The Glorious, Tumultuous, Behind-the-Scenes Story of Ohio State Football*, author Joe Menzer writes, "Woody's father would read six or more books at the same time and leave them lying half-open around the house. The father would study the books himself, leaving the lasting impression with Woody that no one is ever too old to learn something new." In later years, Woody was known as a voracious reader.

In his 1974 biography, *Woody Hayes and the 100-Yard War*, author Jerry Brondfield noted, "He eventually developed such protean tastes in reading that he can be described as a Renaissance man in his versatility and breadth of knowledge."

Even Abner Doubleday, the nineteenth-century military man often credited with inventing baseball (though he himself made no such claim), said of his youth, "I was brought up in a bookstore and early imbibed a taste for reading."

Boxing legend Gene Tunney was a surprisingly cultured man who frequently read from "an eclectic mix of literature . . . [including] books on philosophy, psychology and economics" (*Tunney*, Jack Cavanaugh, Random House, 2006). On the day of his 1927 rematch with Jack Dempsey, the unflappable Tunney "prepped" by reading Somerset Maugham's *Of Human Bondage*. Tunney won that match, by the way. Did books make the difference? Hard to say, but reading sure didn't hurt Gene Tunney.

Books have likewise influenced more than a few well-known sportswriters. Jimmy Cannon was one of America's most beloved sportswriters before his too-early death in 1973, and he was a lifelong reader. "It was my own idea," Cannon once said. "Some of the people in my family were worried I would ruin my eyes." Still, he spent many youthful hours at the public library on Leroy Street in Manhattan.

Red Smith was likely the best-known sportswriter of all time. Biographer Jerome Holtzman quotes Smith as recalling, "My parents read all the time. They weren't scholars, but they were literate. I remember bookcases with glass doors. I read everything in the house . . ." Smith later said of his craft, "Writing is thinking."

One day Bud [Selig's] sixth-grade teacher, Ruth Schlieben, was talking to Marie Selig and told her, "You know your son, all he wants to do is read sports books." Marie responded, "What's wrong with that? He's reading, isn't he?"

—from *In the Best Interests of Baseball?*
The Revolutionary Reign of Bud Selig by Andrew Zimbalist

Putting Their Muscle into Better Minds

My very own beloved NBA, in fact, sponsors a program called Read to Achieve, whose stated goal is to "encourage young people to develop a lifelong love for reading and encourage adults to read regularly to children." Read to Achieve "touches the lives of more than 50 million children a year through public-service announcements and grassroots events" with "the most extensive educational outreach initiative in the history of professional sports."

The Read to Achieve Pledge

Reading is fun and books are cool too;
I will read a book daily to learn something new.
I will learn different words and I will listen in school when
teachers read stories and share reading rules.
I will practice my skills in every way.
Reading is something I will do every day.
Reading offers great adventures to me, reading will
help me be the best I can be.

In accomplishing this goal, the NBA partners with other national programs and sponsors like Reading Is Fundamental, Scholastic, and the Walt Disney Company to work with schools, libraries, and community-based organizations. Together with these associates, including teams and players from the NBA, WNBA, and NBA Development League, they have developed 112 Reading and Learning Centers and an additional 160 Reading Corners throughout the world. That is phenomenal!

Organizations like these flex their well-honed muscles to sponsor events, encourage book donations, and inspire kids to make books a preferred use of their time. It makes me proud and grateful to be associated with them.

Earlier this year, through Read to Achieve, the *Orlando Sentinel* and the Orlando Magic partnered in the "One Book One Community" program, aimed at kids in kindergarten through fifth grade. Students were able to call a storyline and listen to Magic star Dwight Howard read them a book every month.

I am especially proud of the efforts made by the Magic, who offered both financial and inspirational assistance during the 2006 season to eight elementary schools in six counties, resulting in the reading of more than 46,000 books. Their efforts worked so well that, as one school reported, "The students wanted to earn the incentives. Rarely a day went by that at least one student did not ask me when they would get their Magic incentive."

An official from another school wrote us, "I wish more companies would support schools in a similar way. Reading books saved my life at times, and I would not be a teacher today if I did not love to read. Our students now know that they are important to other people because of your program."

Let me tell you, folks, that kind of response—for doing something we all love—really made us proud we had reached out beyond ourselves to impact those young lives.

NBA star Chris Webber is a huge supporter of the Read to Achieve program. "In the summers," Webber told me, "I talk to kids about how reading can take you out of your environment, how reading can take you to wherever you want to be. If you don't like your environment, if you're from a poor neighborhood, you can go to space. If you can't travel, you can go to Africa through a book. You can go to a jungle through a book. You can watch a movie in a book. Whatever you're interested in, there's a book about that—whether it's skillful things, such as cooking or fixing cars, or whether it's science fiction, E.T., or things like that. You can find something that you like."

Ray Allen adds, "Kids learn so much from reading. Reading can take kids places they cannot go on their own. It allows kids to be more intelligent, but it's also enjoyable."

An article in the May 10, 2006, issue of *USA Today* highlighted another chapter in the Read to Achieve program, this one an outreach to young adults, ages sixteen to twenty-four. Through a partnership with Penguin Classics, adults like Becky Hammon of the New York Liberty and NBA professionals like Dwayne Wade, Magic Johnson, and Ray Allen actively read and discuss with audiences classic novels like *Pride and Prejudice* or *Siddhartha.* Wade added that he recently finished a book by Michael Jordan and moved on to one given him by Miami Heat coach Pat Riley. "[Pat] gives a lot of books . . . The main thing about reading," Wade said, "why I wanted to [be a part of this program], is just trying to get young people to read to show even cool people read."

Our program is designed to demonstrate
that the NBA is behind the literary and computer
worlds. You can't win if you are not in the game,
and you cannot get in the game if you can't read.
We receive wonderful feedback from educators
across America who report that the motivational
ability of our players with young
students is extraordinary.

—David Stern, NBA commissioner,
on the Read to Achieve program

I can't tell you how proud I am of all these "cool people" for setting a reading example.

And while you may have long ago heard that a tree grows in Brooklyn, I've got it on good authority that a minor-league baseball team is growing in community status there, as well. The Brooklyn Cyclones, a Mets affiliate, has been actively involved in rallying civic support for baseball and returning the favor through programs like the Cyclones Book Patrol. The book club involves players traveling to local schools to read to the kids during the off-season. But it doesn't stop there. During the season, coaches and players read to the kids before the Sunday games, right there in KeySpan Park.

In sports, as in all walks of life, the interests of its participants run the gamut. I was encouraged by a *Sports Illustrated* survey from the spring of 2006 that highlighted three Houston baseball players that *SI* called the "Smart Astros." Eric Bruntlett graduated from Stanford University with a degree in economics, scored 1,400 (of a possible 1,600) on his SAT, and was reading *Elegant Universe*, a book by physicist Brian Greene, at the time of the interview. Closer Brad Lidge spent three years at Notre Dame and is an ancient civilizations fan, citing Herodotus's *The Histories* as a favorite book. Brad Ausmus, Astros catcher, earned his government degree from Dartmouth. Proving that even baseball players don't fall too far from the family tree, Ausmus's father is a retired history professor who wrote *A Schopenhauerian Critique of Nietzsche's Thought*, a favorite with son Brad. Wow, and I'd be happy if they just read current bestsellers.

As my eyes scanned the bottom of the page in that *SI* article, however, my heart sank. At least two players responded to the question "book I'm currently reading" with, "I don't read." Gentlemen, I hope someone gives you this book and gets you started on a life of dynamic change. No matter how successful we are, all of us can stand to make a little life-altering decision now and then.

Athletes, those of you out there reading this book, you need to know that kids look up to you. They admire you and want to be like you. If you're a star today, you've been given an awesome opportunity to influence lives. Make sure you're a positive force for them. Make sure what they learn about you are qualities they'll want to incorporate in their own lives. You have that much power! Use it wisely. Be like Chris Webber and Ray Allen and Grant Hill and Otis Smith . . . and so many more fine examples. When you're not on the courts or ball fields, let those kids know you read.

---

*When I was a kid growing up in the
DC area, I loved Wes Unseld, Kevin Porter, and
all the Bullets. If they had come to my school
and told me to do something, I'd have done it in
a heartbeat. Athletes can have that effect on
youngsters, and I believe the NBA's
Read to Achieve program is influencing a lot
of youngsters to become readers.*

—Grant Hill, Orlando Magic

The *Who* Factor:
So What Can I Do About It?

If success in life is your goal, and I'm guessing it is, I hope you realize that books are tools to help you get there. As I said at the beginning of this chapter, everyone needs to read in order to get ahead in life. Here are a few critical questions you'll find answers to through books:

1. **Who am I?** This question is one that all of us need to answer for ourselves. The answer may be a lifetime in unfolding, but there are things you can know—and should know—early on. What books help you discover who you are, and what is the purpose of your life?

2. **What do I want to accomplish?** Ben Franklin wrote, "Father's small library consisted primarily of books about religious disputes. I read many of them and later regretted the choice as I was no longer going to become a clergyman." By refining your choices, you can better select those specific books that help you move your ball down the court.

3. **What are my core convictions?** Anyone can have an opinion, and issues are argued every day in almost every place. But what do you believe in? What matters so much to you that you'd be willing to give your life for it? Books can help you give a name to those ideals and values that drive you, that make your heart beat faster and send the blood rushing through your veins.

4. **What things do I do well?** As tempting as it is to want to be "all things to all people," none of us can attain that title. But we can all be good at something. I've discovered that life is about knowing your own shape—sensing what makes your heart race, listening for those moments when others notice your accomplishments, following what you're interested in, serving where you can be the greatest blessing to others. Over time, as long as your primary desire is to do what you've been put on Earth to do, your goals, like Ben Franklin's, will be refined. Books help you find the right words.

5. **What great people do I know?** If you're an entrepreneur, you might wish you were best friends with people like Donald Trump, Bill Gates, or even Ben Franklin. Many of us wish we could rub shoulders with the president of the United States, or some other great and respected leader. But most of us can't actually know those people. So look for people in your world whom you can get to know. What community leader has been an inspiration in your life? You'd be surprised at how approachable some of those people are. Invite them to lunch or out for coffee. Let them know you're looking for a mentor.

In the meantime, let books introduce you to those people of influence you might never meet otherwise. I can't encourage that enough. Biographies, how-to books, success stories—through these pages we can reach across both miles and generations. For all our modern technology and instant messaging potential, books remain the most effective way to be impacted by great hearts and minds.

So now we know why reading is important. We've talked about when to squeeze it into our busy lives. And we know that books introduce us to some terrific people, including ourselves. Even so, I'll concede that maybe, up to now, reading has just never been your "game of the week." Let's take a close look at how to read as if, well, as if it were a question of life or death. I believe it is.

Read for Your Life Way No. 8:

Learn the *How* Factor

14

Read as if Your Life Depends on It

"I really think that the written word is what defines us as superior creatures to all the other creatures on Earth," said novelist and Civil War historian Shelby Foote in an interview with C-SPAN's Brian Lamb. Foote went on to opine that man, as the only animal who knows he's going to die someday, has "an obligation to make the most of whatever time he has. And making the most of it is enormously assisted by reading, by learning about the world."

We need to maximize our moment on this Earth. Ultimately, that's all any of us has—a moment. Books can help us make the most of it.

Read Interactively

Reading, on its surface, is a solitary rather than a social event. With all the choices available to us—movies, video games, sporting events, television, the Internet—reading all too often comes in on the list of "things to do when we have time"—which all too often means never. So what can we do to change that?

In recent years, book clubs and reading groups have become popular, primarily among women. Thanks to superstar advocates like Oprah Winfrey, many are even rediscovering the classics. Using her successful TV show and the Internet, Winfrey has found a way to get America reading—at least that part of America that watches Winfrey's weekday talk show. "The book club is back, and I am on a mission," says Winfrey through her website. "My mission is to make this the biggest book club in the world and get people reading again. Not just reading, but reading *great* books."

Some books take a while to get into.
Others grab you by the heartstrings and whisper,
"You're not going anywhere, honey."

—*O, The Oprah Magazine,* July 2006

Through interactive areas of her website, Winfrey offers an online reading group, where members may ask questions, get answers, and find tips for starting or finding reading groups in their area. I am thankful for people like Oprah Winfrey who go the extra mile to encourage reading. She has set an example that many others, myself included, are following to some degree.

My love of reading is well represented on my website. Others, like radio personality Hugh Hewitt, for example, also offer reading lists. Pat Schroeder, president of the Association of American Publishers, said in a recent interview, "People want to read, but they're overwhelmed by all the choices. They're always excited to have someone steer them."

So if knowing where to get started is a problem for you, visit one of these sites. Then the only problem you'll have is which one to read first!

An article about the Internet's influence on our reading habits caught my eye not long ago. The article focused on the invention by University of Virginia literature professor Jerome McGann and colleagues of a software program that makes reading a truly interactive, as well as a collaborative, event. Ivanhoe, as the program is called, engages students in such activities as rewriting great works of literature, role playing, keeping extensive journals, and reacting to the interpretations of others ("How the Internet Saved Literacy," Maureen Farrell, *Forbes* magazine, December 1, 2006).

Finding ways to make reading a social event may be more challenging than just turning on the TV, but with a little imagination and drive, anyone can do it. Start your own reading group—in your home, your neighborhood, your church, your workplace, your school—wherever you regularly meet with other people. Do you know anyone who wouldn't benefit from reading? I don't.

In our home, Ruth and I have made it a practice over the years to make books central in our lives. When the kids were little, we read aloud to them. (They're all grown up now, but with our houseful, that was a lot of years of reading aloud.) As they got older, and even now, books are the gifts they receive. When I've gone on to that great library in the sky, if there's only one thing my kids will remember about their dear old dad, it's that he loved books.

What will your family and friends remember about how you spent your time? Are you investing it, or wondering where it went?

***

Lincoln never read any other way but aloud.

—William Herndon, Abraham Lincoln's law partner

Read Reflectively

You'll get far more out of what you read if you think of it as having a conversation with the author. Why not keep a reader's notebook? Ask questions, and then write down whatever answers come to you. Make your questions open-ended and explorative: Who? What? Where? When? Why? How?

What you "hear" in response may not be what the author would actually say, but it may likely be how the mystery of communication really works. What I write on this page may connect with your brain in such a way that new ideas are triggered. Words have tremendous candlepower to light our passions and blaze new trails. It's almost magical.

Give it a try. Commit to yourself that for the next year you'll keep a reader's notebook and use it whenever you're reading one of those especially provocative books.

Or write a book review on Amazon.com after you finish your next book. You may be surprised at how this little exercise helps clarify your thinking about what you just read.

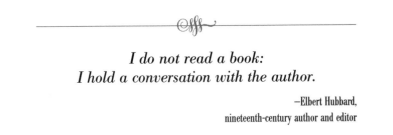

I do not read a book:
I hold a conversation with the author.

—Elbert Hubbard,
nineteenth-century author and editor

Read with a Servant's Heart

In his book, *Why Read?* author Mark Edmundson asserts that the common practice in today's universities of training literature students to critically analyze the works they study often leads to an attitude of superiority over the work itself. This mind-set, as Edmundson sees it, is a byproduct of living in the age of mass consumerism.

That idea intrigues me as one that needs to be confronted and nipped in the bud—eliminated immediately from the program directory. I believe a critical attitude in any walk of life all too often fosters feelings of superiority. Yes, we need to be discerning and understand the works we read, but our attitude should be one of learning from one another, not comparing ourselves to one another.

Rick Warren has said about comparing: "You'll either think yourself worse than someone else, or better than someone else. Neither of these is good. Stop comparing."

Don't let reading make you arrogant. It can happen—believe me. Maybe you've even met a person or two like this, someone who thinks that being an English literature major or particularly well read puts them above the crowd. Take my advice: even if it's true, don't go there.

*I have been learning how to read for
the past fifty years, but have
not yet succeeded.*

—Johann Wolfgang von Goethe,
eighteenth-century writer and German scientist

Prideful thinking is not only false, but it can be downright deadly. Author Greg Morris tells the story of an Avianca Airlines jet that crashed in Spain in 1984. "Investigators studying the accident made an eerie discovery," Morris wrote. "The 'black box' cockpit recorders revealed that several minutes before impact, a shrill, computer-synthesized voice from the plane's automatic warning system told the crew repeatedly in English, 'Pull up! Pull up!'

"The pilot, evidently thinking the system was malfunctioning, snapped, 'Shut up!' and switched the system off. Minutes later the plane plowed into the side of a mountain. Everyone on board died."

Just as with instruments, there are plenty of books out there that can mislead us or give us false indications, but those written by men and women of passion and insight overshadow them. Books issue warnings, and books point us toward truth. They help us to see into the deep—beyond this mere physical world. To ignore their warnings is just as dangerous as to think we already know them.

I urge you to read, knowing the words you absorb will come out in your life in ways that inspire, uplift, and encourage someone else. Life is meant to be passed on. Read with a servant's heart.

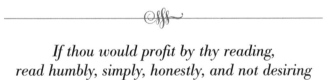

If thou would profit by thy reading,
read humbly, simply, honestly, and not desiring
to win a reputation for learning.

—Thomas à Kempis, fifteenth-century
author of *The Imitation of Christ*

Endless Possibilities

Even if reading doesn't top your personal skill set, there are more options today for getting information from books than ever before in history. Audiobooks and portable listening devices make it possible for almost anyone to read, and their increasing popularity is encouraging.

Jonathan Lowe wrote in *Christianity Today* (June 1, 2006), "Zondervan, the Christian division of HarperCollins, reports a

24-percent increase in audiobook sales in the past two years . . . Time Warner AudioBooks (TWA) is seeking a 10-percent audiobook share of its million-plus hardcover sales . . .

"Anthony Goff, TWA's associate publisher, tells *CT*, 'For a relatively new medium, these are explosive numbers, and now we are attracting younger listeners with new technology . . .'"

Touted as "a new way to borrow audiobooks from the library" involving "no CDs, no car trips, no fines, and no risk of being shushed," a recent Associated Press article by Michael Hill talked about "borrowing" audiobooks from library websites and downloading them to your favorite listening device.

You can buy or borrow books on CD and listen to them during your daily commute to work, or you can download a book directly into your portable listening device. It simply could not be easier to get information from books than it is today.

This is my point: if you've got either two eyes or two ears or two hands that work and you live in America, there is basically no excuse not to benefit from books. Look for ways to maximize your moment on Earth in the pages of a few great books.

15

How to Make Reading a Regular Part of Your Life

There's no doubt about it—activities rule in today's world. It's way too easy to get caught up in the tyranny of the urgent. You've got to schedule reading, just like you book time for exercise, meals, and all the other "dailies" that matter. Because reading matters to me, I've found a way to make it work, in spite of a decidedly packed agenda. Here's a peek at my reading schedule—offered not to intimidate, but to inspire. We all have the same amount of time in a day, so if I can do this, so can you.

I've got reading stacks in just about every room—in my office at work and at home, by the bed. I figure I'm about two hundred and fifty books behind. I've usually got ten or twelve books going at a time—not to confuse myself, but because it keeps my interest alive. It keeps me fresh and sharp as I work through eight or ten different topics. One book might be on sports; another might be on the Civil War; still another might be a biography, a business book, or a book on leadership. I find that if I rotate them, my mind is a lot more into the reading. In addition to the books, I read from at least five newspapers and magazines every day. Not everyone can do this, but I recommend at least giving it a try. You might be surprised to find you enjoy "multitasked" reading.

Another trick that helps is having a goal, a mission in my reading. I set out to finish one book every day. Most days, unless they are extraordinarily unusual, I get three hours of reading in throughout the course of the day. With all the kids out of the house now I can generally get two to two and a half hours sitting at my desk in the evenings. I purposely do not sit in a comfortable chair, or I'll be asleep in five minutes. But if I'm sitting upright at a desk in a desk chair, I can't just sit back and enjoy the reading ride.

Then again, if getting to sleep is a problem for you, try reading yourself to sleep. I continue to read in bed before the lights go out, and that's the best tonic I know to get in your forty winks. I do my serious reading at the desk, and then I read reclining. Sleep comes very quickly that way.

But because I've set a goal, by then I've already got my two-plus hours of reading in, and hopefully I've finished a book. It's a wonderful feeling of accomplishment when I take a book into the big library and put it on the shelf permanently. There it sits. I look at my books as trophies, prominently on display. Each book becomes part of my life. I've spent a portion of my life with it; I've committed to it; and that book, in return, has become part of me.

---

*A library is a token of, nay,
a trophy of grace.*

—Martin Luther

So how does a busy man like me—sports executive, on-the-go public speaker, author, husband, and father of nineteen kids—accomplish this goal? I do it the same way anyone can, the same way *you* can—by doing it. Like any other skill, the more you read, the better you get at it. And the better you get at it, the more you enjoy it, and the more you enjoy it, the more you want to do it. The more you want to do it, the more accomplished you become. It's a cycle that just feeds on itself, with the end result a stronger, more agile mind, a richer vocabulary, and a well-stocked imagination.

I have one small confession to make—and please don't think me too strange. I generally read books from both ends at the same time. When I'm finished, I'm not at the end . . . I'm in the middle. Why do I read like that? I have no idea. It just appeals to me. As I've said elsewhere, books help you discover who you really are.

We only have one lifetime in which to influence others. But by reading and writing books, that influence can span generations far beyond our few years. Be an active part of the fabric of life. Knit yourself into history.

However you use it, once you've finished a book, you are never the same. Your mind has been changed by what you just read. In the chapter on why we should read, we talked about connecting with the mind of the writer. Author Ray Bradbury once said that a trip to Disneyland is like going inside the mind of Walt Disney. What a great visual picture! When we read, we interact with the mind of that author. So make reading a conversation. Take notes! Write the author, if she is still living, and tell her how much her book impacted you.

In the back of all the books I write, I include my e-mail address, mailing address, website, and private phone numbers. I love it when people e-mail or call me to tell me how one of my books touched their heart or opened a window in their mind. Those letters and e-mails are worth more to me than any dollars that the sale of my books may garner. Of course, I pass those e-mails on to my publishers. It validates their wise decision to publish my book!

Before we leave this topic, I want to apprise you of the fact that there are some wrong ways to read, too. By wrong, I mean failing to get the most from what you read. Surface reading is dishonoring to the writer, and what's more, it's dishonoring to you, too. Respect others enough to want to know what they think; respect yourself enough to consider the ideas of others. Speaker and author Mark Eppler cautions us, "Don't skim: read! Reading has fallen on hard times, in a culture conditioned by the Internet to surf and skim. Depth of knowledge and understanding, however, come from really getting into a wide range of topics." If you really want to understand—a topic, a story, or life itself—read thoroughly; read to learn; read to engage your mind.

The *How* Factor: So What Can I Do About It?

I hope by now you're getting the message: books matter. Reading is critical, not only for you, individually, but to our survival as a culture. Your life could very well depend on being able to read!

Books change you. The right book in the right hands challenges you to get up off your sofa and make a difference in your world! So don't just read a book and put it down. Do something with what you just read. I've told you how reading Bill Glass's motivational books sparked my speaking career. I read the books, and then I did something about it. That's how it works. While on its surface reading may seem like a solitary occupation, here are some suggestions for making it an interactive experience:

1. **Read with a positive attitude.** Abraham Lincoln was an avid reader, a passionate reader. Books mattered more to him than any treasure. Earlier we noted that when Abraham Lincoln obtained a long-wanted book, "his eyes sparkled, and that day he could not eat, and that night he could not sleep."

   Have you ever felt that way about a book? Believe me,

I understand old Abe's exhilaration over books. If this idea seems strange or foreign to you, I pray you will decide to take a deeper look.

Look at it this way: if Lincoln was willing to risk his father's wrath and his community's estrangement in order to read books—which he did—there must be something very important about books. Don't you think so? Rather than run from them or put them off for a movie, TV show, or video game, I urge you to dig deeper. Find the gold and jewels that are waiting for you in the pages of a book.

2. **Read with an explorer's sense of wonder.** Keep a notebook and pen or pencil—your reader's equivalent of a GPS and hiking boots—at your side as you read. Take notes on those thoughts and ideas the author's words have sparked. It will make your reading experience more like a conversation with the author. Consider this: an idea is really just a flash, a spark across your mind. If you do nothing with it, it's gone forever. What would have happened if Walt Disney had thought, *A theme park the whole family can enjoy . . . I should build that someday*, and that was as far as it went? Don't let go of that idea, my friend. If it's a good one, you and I may meet one day—at *your* Disneyland or in the pages of your book.

3. **After you've finished, tell others about the book.** Join a reading club or write a review for a site like Amazon.com. Word of mouth is still one of the most powerful immediate sales tools out there, so if you like the book, share the good news!

4. **Let that book become part of your research for a book of your own.** Use that notebook to write down all the topics your reading has inspired.

We only have one lifetime in which to influence others. But by reading and writing books, that influence can span generations far beyond our few years. Be an active part of the fabric of life. Knit yourself into history.

Read for Your Life Way No. 9:

Define the *New You* Factor

16

New Goals for a New You

You are the solution to America's reading crisis. You, and you, and you, and you, and you. Me, too.

Each one of us has to do our part, set the example, engage the process, in order to rescue books before they are trampled into the dust by a stampeding host of diversions that ultimately don't matter.

If high-tech toys have you hooked, think about it this way: books are the ultimate form of wireless communication! No plug-ins, no add-ons, no batteries required—and they're completely portable. They have unlimited memory expansion capabilities, and their power to renew your life exponentially is a story yet to be told. Books update the current version of you with each read. No software to download, no annual licenses to renew.

Now that we've unpacked and examined all the reasons that reading is critical to our lives, I'd like to share what has helped me become a better reader. So get out your pencils and notebooks: we're going to set some new goals.

In the next few pages, I'm going to challenge you to make

reading a regular, scheduled part of your day.

Your job is to take up the gauntlet. As part of your reading warrior training program, we'll demystify the bookstore experience, and I'll pass along some great speed-reading tips I wish I'd learned earlier in life. The great news is, it doesn't matter if you're nine or ninety. If you're still breathing, there is time to impact this world through books.

Action 1: Pat's Lifetime Reading Challenge

I am a reader today because I had parents who read. They set the example. You can do this, too. Here's how:

Starting today, I'm challenging you to make a commitment to read one hour a day, every day, for the rest of your life, from a book. Not from the same book, but from books. You can use the hour any way you want—one sixty-minute session, two thirties, four fifteens, or fifteen fours. You can read six times a day for ten minutes or ten times for six. Thirty twos or sixty one-minute sessions would be fine. I don't care how you do the hour, just make sure you do it. Plan it. Promise me—and, more importantly, promise yourself—that you'll accept this challenge.

If there's a reason you picked up this book, and I believe there is, let it be to turn you into a disciplined daily reader.

There's one stipulation: magazines, newspapers, trade journals, periodicals, devotional material, and romance novels do not count. Read those on your own time. On my time, read from real books. The good news? You get to pick the books. And never pick up a book in which you're not interested.

Why an Hour?

I'm glad you asked. If you read one hour a day, at the end of one week you will finish a book. You say, "Big deal." I say, it's a huge deal, and here's why: the average man, upon finishing high school, will not read another book the rest of his life. Statistics show that women purchase 85 percent of all books bought in this country. Despite the fact that bookstores are popping up almost as fast as McDonald's and Burger King, *only 5 percent* of the American public will ever set foot in a bookstore *in their lives.* You might as well take that other 95 percent and drop them in the jungles of Brazil— they'd be just as lost there as they would be in the lobby of a Barnes & Noble, Borders, Books-a-Million, or a B. Dalton store.

―――――――――――――― ⊘ℰ ――――――――――――――

*When I went to work for W. Clement Stone
in 1969, he sat me down for a one-hour interview.
His first question was, "Do you watch television?"
He then asked me, "How many hours a day do
you think you watch?" After a short calculation
I answered, "About three hours a day."
Mr. Stone looked me directly in the eye and said,
"I want you to cut out one hour a day; reduce
your TV-watching time to two hours per day.
If you do that, you'll be saving 365 hours per year.
If you divide that by a forty-hour workweek,
you'll see that you'll have added about
nine and a half additional weeks of productivity
to your life. That's like getting two
additional months every year!"
I agreed that this was a great leveraging
concept, and then I asked Mr. Stone what he
thought I should do with this extra hour every
day. He suggested I read books in my field . . .
I took his advice and it has made a
profound difference in my life.*

―Jack Canfield,
The Power of Focus (HCI, 2000)

In 2005 alone, an average of more than five hundred books per day were published in the United States. Again, only 5 percent of the American public will buy these books, and 70 percent of those books will never be finished. It's amazing to realize it, but as those statistics we looked at in the first few pages of this book revealed, we live in a nonreading society. Our world is built around television, videos, DVDs, Internet screens, and computer games. All of these devices carry a mentality that says, "Entertain me! Don't make my brain work too hard." Reading's message is, "Challenge me. Push me. Build my brain. Make me think."

Which of these messages is yours? Only you can answer that question. It's my hope, of course, that you choose the disciplined path, the one that leads to stronger minds, and not the one that ultimately stands to doom our culture. Like the message delivered to Ebenezer Scrooge by the spirits of Christmas past, present, and future, it's not too late to change the tide of tomorrow's events. If reading has not been your personal habit up to now, take my reading challenge. Find out how rewarding reading really is. Watch it expand your life; let it introduce you to new ideas . . . and even a few new friends.

Think of it this way: if you will read one hour a day, you will finish a regular-sized book in one week. Keep it up, and at the end of one year, you will have read fifty-two books. Here's an enticing fact to consider: if you read the right five books on any one subject, you will be considered a world-leading authority on that topic. That means, if you so desire, in one year you can become a *world-leading authority* on as many as ten different subjects! Can you hear the media calling you when big news breaks? It could happen.

In late 2006 I spoke about Walt Disney's five secrets of business success (from my book *Go For the Magic*, Nelson, 2005) at the offices of Disney Worldwide Shared Services. Disney "Cast Member" Jay Guthrie wrote me later to say, "I have tried to put your take home point into practice—read one hour each day." Guthrie then confessed his first reading choice was *Don Quixote*—a classic story more than 1,000 pages long! "At least," he added, pointing to Walt's unique term for the principle of persistence, "I will get a chance to practice stick-to-it-ivity." That's *exactly* how it works.

If you read one hour a day, at the end of ten years, you will have finished 520 books, and potentially become a world-leading authority on more than 100 different topics. Do you think that, ten years from today, having become a world-leading authority on 100 topics will make a difference in your life? A difference in your relationships? A difference in your earning capacity? Do you think you could be the most requested lunchtime companion in your community? People will be begging to take you to Olive Garden—and they'll pick up the tab! I'll tell you in advance what their complaint will be: "I couldn't take it all in. There was so much pouring out from your side of the table that I didn't know what to do with it all. I only brought a thimble to lunch, and I should have brought a bucket. What's going on with you?" And then you get to tell them. Just think of it—the lives you will impact—just because you read!

Yes, You Can

Several years ago, famed historian David McCullough was the commencement address speaker at the University of Massachusetts. During his remarks, McCullough said, "I understand the average American watches four hours of television a day. That's twenty-eight hours a week. I also understand the average American reads two hundred and fifty words per minute. Therefore, if the average American would turn off the television set and spend those twenty-eight hours a week reading, he could read all the poems of T. S. Eliot, all the poems of Maya Angelou, two plays by Thornton Wilder, including *Our Town, The Great Gatsby* by F. Scott Fitzgerald, and all one hundred fifty psalms in the Old Testament. That's all in one week. My advice to you, graduates, is read, read, read."

Books are the carriers of civilization.
Without books, history is silent, literature dumb,
science crippled, thought and speculation
at a standstill.

—Barbara Tuchman, writer

Maybe reading is something you struggle with, and if so, I'm truly sorry. But my lifetime in sports has taught me that the old saying "practice makes perfect" is basically true. While nothing in this life is ever quite perfect, you can certainly improve your abilities through practice. I know how frustrating it can be when something you know you ought to do does not come naturally, but I also know that if you truly desire to learn it, you can. So say this along with me: "From now on, 'I can't' is no longer part of my vocabulary, especially when it comes to reading. With practice and perseverance, the answer is 'yes—I can.'"

Our next marker in the reading roadway takes us on a jog around the local bookstore and includes a few speed-reading laps that could just get you voted the most improved in the class. Are you ready to rumble? Tighten up your jogging shoes, and let's go.

17

Practical Pointers for Your Reading Journey

I n my travels, and as I've spoken to audiences on the topic of reading, one factor has risen above many others as a book barricade: people are frustrated by their inability to read faster. While my current goal, as I'm reading seven to eight books at a time, is to complete at least a book a day, it wasn't always that way. I've put to use two major elements to achieve my current reading goals: 1) an unstoppable drive to meet my goals and 2) practice.

Action 2: Your Personal Speed-Reading Course

Not long ago, I shared David McCullough's information about reading statistics, noted a few pages ago, at a business breakfast in Charleston, South Carolina. Afterward, a woman named Margaret Cotton introduced herself to me.

"Do you realize the average American reads at the sixth-grade reading level?" she asked.

"In other words," I replied, "a sixth-grade reader could consume all of what David McCullough was talking about?"

"Yes. Yes, indeed," Margaret said.

Margaret then explained to me that she'd spent fifteen years teaching reading skills for the Evelyn Wood Reading Dynamics company, a firm whose name was at one time synonymous with what it taught—speed-reading.

I asked Margaret, "How quickly can the average good reader read? An educated person?"

*If I were running a university, I would insist
that these three things be taught:*

1. Memory Training
2. Speed-Reading
*3. How to Recognize Opportunities and Take
Advantage of Them*

—Rich Wolfe, author

Without flinching, she responded, "Seven hundred and fifty words per minute. And up to 1,000 words per minute if you're reading in your field."

I did some quick mental math and said, "So you could triple or quadruple the amount of material David McCullough was talking about to those graduates?"

"That's what I'm saying," she said.

By now, Margaret had me hooked.

"Would you share with me the three main reading concepts that you taught your students?" I asked her.

"Pull up a chair," she said, "and get a piece of paper."

Like an obedient student, I did Ms. Cotton's bidding. And now I share these transformational learnings with you:

1. **Use your finger or a pen to keep your eyes focused on the page.** Even though your teachers told you not to do this, do it anyway. They'll never find out. The number-one problem with reading is loss of focus. Your eyes wander all over the page. As you're going down the page, run your finger or a pen down the middle to keep your eyes focused on the page. It's important that you do this.

2. **Read fast.** If you want to run fast, you practice running fast. If you want to throw a baseball fast, you practice throwing fast. Therefore, if you want to read fast, practice reading fast. Your brain can absorb information a lot faster than your eyes can deliver it. If your brain is not getting fed fast enough, it gets very bored and shuts down. Therefore, to keep your brain engaged, you must be pumping information through your eyes as fast as you can. Don't worry about retention at this point. It will come. Work on reading as fast as you can.

3. **Use your full field of vision.** Most people read across the line one word at a time. If you keep on doing it that way, you'll be reading that one book forever. The mission is to get down the page, not across it. Therefore, using your peripheral vision, grab chunks of words at the same time—phrases, short sentences, small paragraphs—flushing the information from your eyes back to your brain as fast as you can to keep your brain fully engaged.

With those amazing words of advice from Margaret Cotton, my day—*my year*—was made. I raced off to the Charleston airport, knowing I was on to something; I only wished I had met Ms. Cotton forty years earlier. By putting her tips to work for me, my reading skills improved immediately, and continue to improve to this day. Reading is a skill, and like any other skill, you must understand the fundamentals, practice them faithfully, and be consistent in their execution. The more you practice hitting a golf ball the right way, the better you get. The same game goes for serving a tennis ball. *Reading is no different.* The more you work at it, the better you get.

If you are an average reader (220 words a minute) and read just twenty minutes a day, in a year you will have read twenty 200-page books.

—Zig Ziglar, motivational speaker

My personal goal is to read three to four hours a day and finish at least one book a day for the rest of my life. My life revolves around my reading habits. When I'm reading, I always carry a pen and mark the passages and quotes that I consider valuable. Later I will make copies of those marked portions and file them away by topic to use in my own speaking and writing projects.

Now you know the secret, too. What are you going to do with it? Maybe you're thinking, *Okay, Pat. I get the picture, and I'm ready to try. But I still haven't got my next book picked out.* Surprise! The bookstore is the next stop on our list.

Action 3: How to Navigate a Bookstore

There are all kinds of book lovers. They run the gamut from the romantic to the practical, and even the playful. I am a practical reader. I want my books to be useful, to teach me things I can use daily and pass on to others in my life. Thankfully, in this great goulash of life, there is room for us all. And to us, the true book lovers, these words of the late novelist Italo Calvino strike a chord: "A bookstore is like a treasure house, storing up all the wisdom of the ages, all the adventures of a lifetime, and all the sensual delights of the moment, for it is in a bookstore that all the shared experiences of literate man are assembled and disseminated for all who have eyes to see, ears to hear, and minds to conceive."

Bookstores are indeed treasure-houses. They are also often launching pads. Until we enter one, we never know what adventures await our hungry hearts.

———————————— ⌾ℳℳ~ ————————————

*Among [Stonewall Jackson's] first steps were
regular visits to New York bookstores.*

—James I. Robertson, Jr., biographer

In recent years, the rise of virtual stores such as Amazon.com, BarnesandNoble.com, and Christianbook.com have created a paradigm shift in the book business, for merchants and consumers alike. Today, we can browse the stalls and buy our books online, rather than standing in line. And for those who find bookstores overwhelming, it's certainly an option.

Somehow, though, I'm confident that no matter what the future holds for e-commerce, brick and mortar bookstores are here to stay. They may be morphing from the dusty old "shoppes," run by dustier old booksellers, into megastores, but they'll continue to be part of the fabric of American life. I could almost guarantee that on my personal participation alone! My visits to the local Borders near my home average three a week. You could say I know my way around a bookstore.

If bookstores are like a foreign land to you, your feelings about going into one may be closer to fear, intimidation, or even sheer terror. The phrase "it's a jungle out there" comes to mind.

I can relate to that. I've been in a few unfamiliar places—and I've survived. Since this is one place I'm very familiar with, let me take a moment or two to offer my services as your personal guide—"your jungle cruise director," as they say at the Disney theme parks. If your pith helmet is secured, let's go. I promise, you won't regret this trip. Unlimited worlds await you!

I went to a bookstore and asked the saleswoman, "Where's the self-help section?" She said if she told me, it would defeat the purpose.

—George Carlin, comedian

One More Thing . . . Before You Walk In

When you make a commitment to become a reader, it's not a casual thing. I read. It's my hobby and avocation; it's what I do. As a reader, I've also become a student of the industry, so I know that, even with a 10 percent decline reported in 2005 new titles, on average there are over 170,000 new books published each year—and that's not counting the rising numbers of books that are self-published. Each of those titles averages sales of about 6,000 copies, total. Not much when you think about it. That's why this first step is critical. I want to help unlock the doors on those difficult reading choices for you, so let me tell you how I make mine.

This is critical: you must have an interest! If you're not passionate, you'll never be able to fake it. Over my lifetime, I've developed a veritable Christmas list of interests, and each one of those has been brought to life by books. Here's what I mean:

Baseball

When Dad gave me that Pop Warner book that started it all, there was no stemming the tide. My collection of baseball books began during my boyhood, with those used books I found in New York. I may not have become a major-league player, but those books without doubt inspired my lifetime career in professional sports.

Abraham Lincoln

Over the years, I've visited almost all the major Civil War sites and read every book on the life of Lincoln I can find. You'd think a point would come where you run out—that there are no more books to be written. But people still buy them and read about old Abe—they're the folks in line behind me.

Mountain Climbing

In the mid-1990s, I took a bold step. And then I took another, and another, and another—all the way up Mount Rainier. It's the only time I went mountain climbing on a grand scale, but it got my blood pumping on that topic. I became absolutely fascinated with mountain climbing, appreciative of it, fascinated by it. To this day a good mountain book comes, and I'm probably in the middle of it—all because of having ascended that one time.

Public Speaking

Speaking opportunities first began to come my way in the 1970s, when I was general manager of the Chicago Bulls. As I got more invitations, I wanted to improve. I already knew the best way to do that was to study the masters—the best speakers, the best teachers. So hardly a book comes out on public speaking in which I'm not immersed. If I only learn one or two little things that might help me, it's worth it. My passion for this topic even led to a book on public speaking that my wife, Ruth, and I wrote in 2005 called *Turn Boring Orations into Standing Ovations*.

Walt Disney, Jackie Robinson, and Coach Wooden

What do these three men, from vastly different areas of expertise, have in common? All are legendary men whose lives have deeply impacted mine. In fact, I've written a book about each one of them. When I wrote *How to Be Like Walt, How to Be Like Jackie Robinson*, and *How to Be Like Coach Wooden*, I became intrigued with the lives of these legends. As part of my research, I tracked down every single written word I could find about them. I don't think there's one word written about Coach Wooden that I haven't found.

What I want you to grasp is that reading interests come from life interests. You've got to be immersed in life. You're never too old to create new interests, as I learned climbing Mount Rainier, and when you have an interest, you want to learn about it. The best way to learn is to read. If you have no interests, no curiosity, it's going to be tough for you to be a reader. You cannot read in fields in which you're not interested. It's too tough an assignment.

What topics rivet you? When I go into a bookstore, I know I can eliminate fiction right off the top. I don't read fiction. That's not a judgment, mind you, just a personal preference. My areas of interest are these: sports, naturally; business—specifically, leadership and management; Christian inspiration—we can all become more like our role models; self-help; current events; American history; biography. So that's where I go. I don't go to the computer section or the gardening section. I don't wander, and I don't spend time in sections in which I'm not interested.

I feel so incompetent when I walk into a bookstore. There's so much there that I don't know. Education teaches you to read, and reading is a way for you to educate yourself. It's important, more so today, because society is changing.

—Fisher DeBerry, Air Force football coach

So before I even walk into that bookstore, I already have in mind what I'm after. If you're not sure what that is, ask yourself these questions:

- **What am I interested in?** Is there a topic you'd like to know more about? A field of study you'd like to explore? Or maybe you're already a recognized leader in your arena, but you want to know what other leaders are saying in order to a) support their message; b) correct their message; or, c) identify and prepare to meet areas their message is missing.

- **Where do I need to improve my skills?** What would you like to be able to do better? Maybe you know you need to develop an area of your life, as I did with public speaking back when I first discovered the book by Bill Glass. You'd love to go to those seminars, but who can afford them? Well, guess what? Many of those seminar leaders have written books containing the information you'd get from a costly seminar. Peter Drucker, for example, is justifiably recognized as the kingfish, the guru of contemporary leadership thinking. Though he left this world not long ago, his thoughts are still with us—in the many books he left behind on leadership. Maybe you missed the man, but you don't have to miss his message. Think about what you're burning to know, then look for a category it might fit into once you're in the store. Spend a few bucks on a book or two, and you'll get all the information you'd have gotten from the seminar. You've just gotten it more directly. Instead of listening hard and racing to take notes, it's all there in the book. Open the book, open your mind, and pour it in.

- **How can I do my job better or train myself for the career I really want?** Maybe you've got your degree, and you're using it every single day. But life is not static. What we learn in school is great, but we've got to keep up our skills, keep watching the market to see where it's headed, keep our fingers on the pulse for the next paradigm shift to come along.

If we don't, we'll find ourselves washed out by a wave we didn't see coming. Books are like surfboards for our brains.

• **Where do I need inspiration?** Maybe you just need new ideas. We all do sooner or later. Here's one of the more exciting things I've discovered about books: they allow you to have a brainstorming session all by yourself! There have been times I was reading, alone in a room at home, when an idea from a book just grabbed on to my brain like a power surge, and I'd leap out of the chair, shouting, "Yes! *That's* what we need to do!" My wife, Ruth, wondered who I was talking with, until she realized it was just Pat, reading again.

• **Where do I want truth?** There is no question that today's media has an agenda, and most of it involves capturing our minds. Once they've got us where they want us, who knows what fate is in store for our nation? So you and I have an obligation to learn the truth. What is really going on in this world? Here's where you're going to have to do a little trusting and a lot more discerning—but I have faith in you. Bookstores are filled with books to help you sort out the chaff from the wheat.

Decide in advance that you won't waste time on topics that don't interest you. Unless you have a lot of spare time (a rarity these days), that advance-planning strategy helps you resist the temptation to start wandering around the store. I can't stress that enough.

There's something special about
people who are interested in the printed word.
They are a species all their own—learned,
kind, knowledgeable, and human.

—Nathan Pine, bookseller

Remember, too, that every bookstore has employees who can help you find your way around. I've even heard they don't bite, though they might foam at the mouth a little over their personal favorites—especially if they've just downed a cappuccino from the store's coffee central on their break.

Ready? Let's go on inside.

What's in Store?

The first thing I do when I get to the store is make a beeline for the front table where the new books are. If 190,000 new books are published every year, how many do you suppose arrive each day? That front table changes every day, sometimes twice a day. Once those books leave that table and go back to the archives, they may disappear forever. That's an almost unbearable thought!

Now remember those questions? Time to pull out that sheet of paper on which you wrote them and start looking.

- **What am I interested in?** Is there a book on the new-arrivals table that might fit? If not, now's the time to begin getting familiar with those long rows of books. Pick your topic and head on over to the information desk to find out where those books are located. It's right over there.

- **Where do I need to improve my skills?** I'll always be grateful to those books by Bill Glass for building an area of my life that has become one of the most rewarding. Speaking has plussed my life in ways I could never have imagined if I'd continued to make excuses for my lack of a message. And in time, if I hadn't figured out what that message was, my phone would have stopped ringing long ago. Today, because I speak, I travel the country, meet fascinating people, reconnect with old friends, share my enthusiasm in ways that light fires in others—the list goes on. Books can help you find new life opportunities and passionate life messages, too. Look for those books while we're here. And don't worry about me. While you're looking, I'll just be over in the history section, looking for book number 251.

- **How can I do my job better or train myself for the career I really want?** Check to see if there are books that help you predict trends in your field—and get out in front of that wave we talked about earlier. Ever heard that old saying, "Don't prepare for the job you have; prepare for the one you want"? There are reasons old sayings get old—they've proven to be true. So take a look down that row. Don't worry; I'll wait . . . right over there, in the sports section.

- **Where do I need inspiration?** Are you a writer, an artist, a musician? Books are rich sources of ideas for your next project. Or perhaps what you need most is hope in a dark, painful area of your life. Somewhere in here, there's a book to meet you, right where it hurts. No matter what you're experiencing, someone has been where you are and can shed light on your darkness. I can promise you that. Light has warming, comforting, and even healing properties . . . so let someone else's pain bind up your broken heart and point you to the hope you need.

- **Where do I want truth?** Look for books that give you facts and insights on issues from a variety of perspectives. Challenge yourself to think differently—open your mind to new ideas. I love what motivational guru Fred Smith says: "I get a lot of my ideas from synthesizing things from different disciplines." Don't be afraid to go outside the box in your search. Read, read, read—and let the innate intelligence within you synthesize it all. Let books verify truth in your life.

Ready to check out? That wasn't so bad, was it? Maybe I'll even see you here next time I'm in . . . probably in a couple of days.

Staying in the Game

Serious readers *need* to know what's going on. So in between trips to the bookstore, I keep up with the industry by paying attention to the latest information. I read the Sunday *New York Times Book Review,* and then the Thursday *USA Today* section where they feature book news. I also subscribe to *Publishers Weekly* to stay current with trends and news—important for someone who reads and writes books like I do. I recommend them all.

There's a wonderful sense of accomplishment when you walk in those bookstores and see books that you've already read. You look at them and know you're already friends. When I see books in the store that I know have earned a permanent place on my finished reading shelf, I receive a great sense of satisfaction.

As an author, I can relate to the thoughts of contemporary poet Tristan Gylberd, who has observed, "There is no greater delight for an author than to stumble upon a copy of one of his own books in an unfamiliar bookshop. Of course, the comfort and consolation is soon dissipated when he discovers, to his dismay, that he has far more books in hand to purchase than he can ever hope to sell in that little place."

When books are your passion, it's really not such a bad problem to have.

Bookstores today are undergoing a positive change, brought on largely by the Starbucks phenomenon. When these amazing little coffee shops began popping up on every corner, it was only a matter of time before enterprising business owners saw the obvious connection: if you want people to spend time in your store, add a Starbucks. The "relax with us" message Starbucks has mastered, in almost direct opposition to the caffeine jolt they sell, has made them community hangouts, or as one writer put it, "America's new front porch." Thanks to their now-expected presence in Barnes & Noble stores, Starbucks has transformed the bookstore into what *Orlando Sentinel* columnist Kathleen Parker calls "the new public library."

*A bookstore is a place where we can really
have relationships with people
for their entire lives.*

—Stephen Riggio, CEO of Barnes & Noble
(*New York Times*, April 15, 2006)

Here's another power being wielded by today's bookstore: buyers and distributors are rapidly becoming today's market decision-makers. These savvy sellers know what people are buying and will make decisions about what to carry in their stores based on those numbers. Publisher Brian Lewis understands this relationship, which is why he took his unknown title *Has Anyone Seen Christmas?* to Barnes & Noble buyer Brian Monahan in September 2005. Because he knew the work of Lewis and his author wife, Anne Margaret Lewis, he bought the book—and it became one of the breakout Christmas children's books of that year. If you're in the business, it's good to get to know those book buyers.

There's one more thing I do after I've made a great discovery in a bookstore: I tell people about it. When I read a book that excites me, I post the information on my website, tell my friends, family, and associates, or I talk about it when I speak in public. Please feel free to visit my site (www.patwilliamsmotivate.com) frequently for suggestions. You just might find a challenging title or two that will help you see life in a new way. Expanded thinking is always a good thing.

Before we walk out of the store, I want to share a little good news I read recently in a *New York Times* interview (April 15, 2006) with Barnes & Noble CEO Stephen Riggio. "Reports of the book industry's demise have been greatly exaggerated over the last twenty years," Riggio said. "And they've been unsupported by any sound research."

I don't know about you, but remarks like that from industry-leading experts definitely recharge my reading batteries.

Action 4: Your Library Card—
Don't Leave Home Without It

One of the other great benefits of reading is it doesn't have to cost you a lot of money. Oh, it can! Would anyone else out there like to give a testimony on that? Yes, reading certainly can cost you money if you have a habit like mine to support.

But taking out a second mortgage on your home or giving up your kids' college-education fund is not necessary to make reading books a healthy, happy, lifetime pursuit. Thanks to men like Benjamin Franklin, our nation is populated with public libraries. When Franklin and his Junto cronies created the first public libraries, they made books accessible to more people. Before those libraries came into existence, only people of means were able to afford them, limiting education to only certain people. We owe a great debt to old Ben, in so many ways. Next time you pick up a book, think of Ben Franklin and thank him.

Planning a trip to the library is a great opportunity for making lists of all the books you want to read. Keep it handy and take it with you every time you visit the library. When you find a book on your list, make sure to check it off, and keep on adding new titles. And last I heard, library cards were free. Of course, the fines you'll pay for letting your book return date go by can add up, but as I see it, it's all the more reason to make use of that speed-reading course.

---

*When we are collecting books, we
are collecting happiness.*

—Vincent Starrett, book collector and author

When you walk into your local library, don't be dismayed if the current bestsellers aren't there just yet. Wait long enough, and they will be.

Libraries are set up a little differently than bookstores, but once you get the hang of it, locating just the book you want is not difficult. And if the title you had in mind is checked out this week, there's likely another joyful discovery nearby.

In the late 1800s, a librarian by the name of Melvil Dewey invented a system of categorizing library books using decimals. We know that system today as the Dewey decimal classification system, and it is used by all public libraries in the United States. This system makes books pretty easy to find once you've identified the overall category to search.

Inside your library, you'll find card catalogs to help you locate the books you want and, in most cases, banks of computers to help you find them even faster. Plug in the title, author, or category, and within seconds you'll know a) whether or not the library has that book; b) its on-loan status; and c) exactly where you'll find it on the shelves. You'll see a number that will look something like this: 813.45. That is the book's Dewey decimal name, and means that on one side of it you're likely to find book 813.44, and on the other side book 813.46. See? Nothing to it. Typically, that system follows last name of the author, another helpful tool in finding your book.

This is where I confess that, as familiar as my face is at my neighborhood Borders, I'm not well known to my local public librarian. My disadvantage where libraries are concerned is that I like to mark up my books and photocopy key information from them. I can't do that with library books. In spite of that, I'm grateful to old Ben for giving America its fine network of public libraries. What a vast treasure-house of books they make available to us—for free!

───────────────── ⚜ ─────────────────

Getting my library card was like citizenship.
It was like American citizenship.

—Oprah Winfrey

───────────────────────────────────────

Libraries are great places to take kids. Introduce them at a young age to the rich smell of bookbinding, the feel of paper, the weight of that book in their hands. Let their eyes dance over the letters on the pages, even when they're too young to know what those letters represent. They'll want to know soon enough, and this exposure reinforces reading as an essential, fulfilling part of life.

If you haven't been to the library in a while, why not make it your next outing? You might come home with a few new treasures. Trips to the library are an American tradition. As Jennifer Moses suggested in her May 15, 2006, article for the *Atlanta Journal-Constitution*, "To put it plainly: Democracy needs readers. Want to show your patriotism? Forget the flag-waving, and take your kids to the library instead."

Knowing how to read, after all, is only half the conquest. Finding books to read, knowing where they are and how to get them, is the thrill of the hunt. Somehow, I think old Ben must have realized the power in an educated public back when it was his goal to make them part of the American landscape. Thanks for seeing it through, Ben!

Before we leave the library, I want to share a story I happened on recently that makes my case very well. It involves a librarian who was dutifully checking in books when she looked up to see a chicken on her counter. Having caught her eye, the chicken squawked, "Book, book, book, BOOK!" Surprised, the librarian put a small stack of books in front of the bird, who grabbed them and left the building. This scene repeated itself for several days in a row. Finally, the librarian's curiosity could take it no longer. One day, she followed the chicken all the way to a large park. He waddled to the pond and stopped. She crept as close as she could and found the chicken next to a small frog. Together, they carefully examined each book, and the frog said, "Read it, read it, read it . . ."

There you have it, my friends. If even the chickens and frogs are checking books out of the library, what is your excuse?

The *New You* Factor: So What Can I Do About It?

By now, it's my hope you've already begun to do something about it. You've taken my reading challenge, and you're committed to that hour a day. In time, you'll begin to naturally weed out those books that muddle your thinking from those that inspire you. As your reading skills improve, your language and thinking skills are sharpened in the bargain. Set these goals for yourself, and you'll soon see a new you taking shape:

1. **Accept my reading challenge!** I've issued a call to action and rallied the reading troops. The question is no longer "what *can* I do about it?" but "what *are* you *going* to do about it?" I'm guessing there might be a book or two in your home you've always intended to read. Go get them down off the bookshelf now. I'll wait.

   Good. Now put them in the stack by your reading chair, ready to dig into one after you've finished this one. With books, as with any project, I've discovered the best thing to do is always have the next one waiting in the wings. Maybe you understand the phenomenon of letdown that often occurs when you've finished something amazing, something into which you've poured your heart, mind, and strength. One almost surefire way to bounce out of that low spot is to quickly engage in a new endeavor. So have that next book handy and ready to go. Of course, you should definitely take time after each book to reflect on what you just read and decide how to apply it to your life. But once that action plan has been made and you've folded it into the new you, get going on the next book.

2. **Exercise daily.** Regular workouts not only strengthen your body, they are critical wherever you desire excellence in your life. If you want to get better at anything, you've got to practice it daily. Knowing how to read is only one step toward conquering illiteracy. We all know how to eat, but unless we know where to go for food, we'll surely die of malnutrition. Whether you choose the bookstore, the public library, or your own private selection, know where to go for your daily workout sessions.

3. **Recognize why reading goals—and all goals—matter.** Entertainer John Morgan wrote me, "Reading is right! I have grown in many ways . . . through my reading and study of valuable books. I have fallen short of my reading one hour minimum per day," Morgan confessed, "but at the very least I have a goal, and I have read vastly greater amounts than I would otherwise have done without it."

   So actually achieving your goals isn't necessarily why you need to make them. Goals are like targets. They are like destinations on a map—in this case, the map of your life. They focus your vision and energy on what you want to accomplish. You may or may not reach all those goals. In truth, most of us reach some of them. Few of us reach all of them. But without a goal, you'll be like the guy who got in his car and just started driving. Because he never knew where he was headed, he ended up stranded on the road, out of gas, and lost. Don't get lost! Books, by the way, are great tools for adjusting those road markers and compass headings.

   Speaking of reading goals, both *U.S. News & World Report* and the *Wall Street Journal* ran articles in 2006

about President Bush's decision that year to enter a
book-reading competition with advisor Karl Rove.
You can't tell me the president of the United States isn't a
busy man—but he recognizes the importance of books to
staying educated, and of goals to reach destinations.
Writer Kenneth T. Walsh (*U.S. News & World Report*,
August 17, 2006) more than gently implied Bush's reading
competition was an attempt to improve his less than
scholarly image. Perhaps that factored in to his motivation,
but at least he recognizes that books offer a direct route
to greater knowledge, and he's set a reading goal.

4. **Rehearse your reading.** Everything we do, even those
things we do well, can be improved upon. Take those tips
from Margaret Cotton and begin applying them in your
daily reading. Even if you do your reading on the computer
screen, there are ways to employ these pointers. In fact, a
pointer is one of them. Take a thin stick of some kind—
a pen, pencil, small pointer, or even the built-in cursor—
and use it to guide your eyes down the screen.

5. **Practice speed-reading during your hour a day.** Keep
track of how your daily quota increases as you practice
what you've learned in this chapter. There is something
both exhilarating and challenging about seeing yourself
improve.

While writing this book, I grew wild-eyed with amazement over an article I spotted in the *Wall Street Journal*
about revived interest in the Evelyn Wood method I
described earlier. Specifically, the article said, it is catching
on with businesspeople "trying to cope with information
overload" (Shivani Vora, July 25, 2006).

The Leaders and Success section of *Investor's Business
Daily* recently featured an article on the value of reading
faster. In it, they recommended a book called *Speed
Reading for Professionals* (Bernard Wechsler and Arthur

Bell, Barron's Educational Series, 2005). Acknowledging the growing reading load of today's professionals, the article advised that when reading, we should take special note of: place (comfortable with good lighting); pacing (using that finger or pen trick I gave you to keep from letting your mind wander); progress (avoid the temptation to go backward, even if you're afraid you missed something—you'll likely pick it up later); paper (that notebook I recommended to write down important points); and an interesting tip called palm, or "fist notes" to keep track of the "who, what, where, when, and how of what you're reading" ("Read Faster, Learn More," *Investor's Business Daily*, December 11, 2006).

You can imagine my joy at seeing the same tips I've shared with you here reinforced in these articles. Practice them daily. I believe you'll be amazed at how your reading improves.

6. **Look for ways to retain what you read.** This can be a tricky step, even for a practiced reader like me. I was grateful for these tips I found in a book by Rick Rusaw (*60 Simple Secrets Every Pastor Should Know*, Group Publishing, 2002). Even though it is directed at pastors, the book contains great practical tips for anyone who finds themselves frequently asking, "Now where did I read that?" Rusaw recommends:

   - Writing the beginning of the sentence and the page number in the back of the book, and even summarizing the idea if it helps. That trick makes it easy to find a source or quote when you need it.
   - Rusaw also likes to use a system of hieroglyphics, his own personally devised code, to identify major topics. Just as Rusaw did, you can develop a system that works for you.

The idea is to identify a method that helps you remember—
and use it!

7. **Take a trip this week to your local bookstore or to the
   library.** Practice those techniques we discussed. Make it
   a point to go at least once a week or once a month to a
   bookstore or library. Before long, you'll be navigating
   those aisles like one born to the purpose. In time, you'll be
   the one giving the guided tours. What better way to pass
   on the joy of reading than to help others make the same
   discovery! Yes, publishers and authors definitely appreciate
   your business . . . but it goes way beyond that. Acquiring
   books, reading them, and then placing them in your home
   library is like creating a blueprint of your mind. And you
   get to be the draftsman! Start that custom design today.

   Whether you read from a book in your hands or from
   an electronic version on your desk or laptop, with practice,
   you can read faster and retain more. While you're setting
   goals, why not make a weekly reading goal? Maybe a book
   a week, or if you're already good at it, maybe two. If even
   one sounds like an impossible dream to you, set that goal
   anyway. You'd be amazed at what the power of a dream
   can do.

8. **Build a home library.** No personal possessions will
   satisfy you more than those books. Every time you walk
   into that room, it's like a family get-together, but without
   the cooking, cleaning, or arguments. Cicero said, "A room
   without books is like a body without a soul." I fully grasp
   that meaning. As our soul is the basis for our personality,
   so books inform that soul. They help make us who we are.
   Books are like the secret ingredients, without which your
   cake recipe would fall flat and tasteless. Whether you buy
   your books at a local bookseller, from Amazon.com, or
   from one of the thousands of used bookstores rapidly

growing in popularity, build a personal library. Nothing quite tells the story of your life like the books you love to read.

So do the math: one hour each day in a book, plus regular trips to your local bookstore or library to round out your reading stack, plus daily practice at improving your reading skills, equals a you who is better equipped to 1) do almost anything you want to do, and 2) be a personal part of the solution to America's reading crisis.

Now that we've cracked the how-to codes for daily reading, and bookstore and library navigation, let's explore ways to impact our world far into the future with this newfound love of words. Turn the page with me and step into tomorrow.

Read for Your Life Way No. 10:

Share the *Beyond* Factor

18

Multiplying Your Influence

In the popular Disney/Pixar *Toy Story* films, action-hero Buzz Lightyear rockets himself into flight with this self-propelling philosophy: "To infinity—and beyond!" That, of course, is an oxymoron. It can't be done! But the challenge is there, nevertheless, friends. We can all do *something* that lives beyond our mere mortal lives.

So picture in your minds what that something might be, and then imagine what it would look like multiplied by a factor of infinity. One life *can* have that power. If I didn't believe that, I wouldn't be writing this book. In this chapter, we'll examine three ways you can—and must!—live this kind of life, and how books help you do that.

Seventeenth-century poet John Donne once penned these profound and classic words that illustrate my point: "All mankind is of one author, and is one volume; when one man dies, one chapter is not torn out of the book, but translated into a better language; and every chapter must be so translated . . . No man is an island, entire of itself . . . any man's death diminishes me, because

I am involved in mankind; and therefore never send to know for whom the bell tolls; it tolls for thee."

What Donne recognized, hundreds of years before we became globally connected through mass media and the Internet, is that none of us—not one person on Earth—lives a completely isolated life. Why else would we experience so much joy when a new life arrives—or so much sorrow when someone we've known and loved leaves this life for the next? We are connected throughout time by the common bond of humanity.

So while we're here, it's critical we leave our mark on those lives around us now, and for those who come after us.

There is no way to know just when the eternity train is coming to pick us up. Will we go before our kids, or after them? So invest in every life now, while you still can.

Two ways we can make those deposits regularly are through inspiring others to read, and by making sure our own stories are carried boldly into the future.

Action 5: Leave a Reading Legacy

Earlier, I told you how my young life was dramatically impacted by a book called *Pop Warner's Book for Boys*. I received that book before I was ten years old, but I remember it to this day because of how it influenced me way back then. Glen Scobie "Pop" Warner, for those of you too young to know the name, was a famous college football coach. In the early 1930s, he and Philadelphia factory owner Joe Tomlin began the Pop Warner Conference youth programs to offer organized sports as an alternative to vandalism for kids who needed redirection in their lives. Pop Warner would have been the Joe Paterno or Bobby Bowden of his day. Though Pop himself is long gone, Pop Warner youth programs are still active today. That's quite a legacy.

Pop Warner's Book for Boys taught youngsters how to live life successfully, so I suppose it qualifies as an early motivational book. One statement in this book really got my attention: Pop Warner wrote that athletes do not smoke, and they do not drink. I was shocked, years later, to find out that was *not* an entirely accurate statement. But to a seven- or eight-year-old, oh, that made sense! It made a tremendous impression on me. According to the great Pop Warner, if I wanted to be an athlete, it meant no smoking and no drinking. To this day I have never touched a drop of alcohol, nor have I smoked a cigarette. Is it because of *Pop Warner's Book for Boys* and its influence on the young Pat Williams? It may well have been.

Read aloud to a child, and you become
a child, listening to the words, as you speak.
Who, then, is really doing the reading?
Your mother, perhaps, or her father?
Down the generations, and over the water
and beyond, the words that create and sustain
civilizations make their way back into the past.
The story you tell, and the story of your
telling it, become words spun from sugar . . .
or thin air . . . into bridges.

—Roger Rosenblatt, essayist

Here's what I'm driving at: books influence our lives at all ages and stages. Parents, if you're concerned about what your kids are doing, who they're hanging out with, what they're watching or listening to in those moments you're not around to monitor their moves, I can't encourage you enough to look for those people, the Pop Warners of this world, who've written books to inspire young minds and hearts. It means you'll have to do some homework and pay attention to who those role models are, but future generations will thank you for making that investment of your time. And your parental conscience will thank you, too.

For those of us whose goal is to get others reading more, it's going to take some creative thinking to help them make this choice. In order to influence others, we must begin by setting the example.

Ruben Martinez, of Orange County, California, is one man who has done this. In September 2004, Martinez was awarded the MacArthur Fellowship—an award of $500,000—for promoting literacy among the children of his community. How did he do it? According to a report in the *Orange County (California) Register*, Martinez began igniting a passion for reading from his neighborhood barbershop when he placed a small book concession in his business. Before long, he'd opened his own bookstore and art gallery, and become one of the largest sellers of Spanish-language books in the country. I'm sure if you could interview him, Ruben Martinez would tell you the money and recognition were nice, but the real reward is in the lives changed by simply encouraging people to read.

Anyone can do this. You do not need to be a wealthy philanthropist with a lot of money to invest in fellowship programs. I've said it before and I'll say it again to underscore its importance . . . I read today because of my mom and dad. Do what they did—set the example by reading in front of your kids. It may not sound like an action-hero thing to do, but it is. Just because the action isn't outwardly visible doesn't mean it's not happening. When you work out, can you see your muscles getting firmer with each weight you pump? I think you get my meaning. Kids learn by what they see, far more than from what they're told.

A children's book is any book
a child will read.

—Madeleine L'Engle, *Walking on Water*

When I'm at home, I'm usually reading a book. I keep one in my office at work and in my car, but home is where I get most of my reading done. My kids know that; my wife knows that. Whenever they ask, "Where's Dad?" they know the answer is likely to be, "Reading."

I can think of no more fitting way to end this section than by paying tribute to my dear "Reading Mother," with these words from Strickland Gillilan's poem of the same name:

> You may have tangible wealth untold;
> Caskets of jewels and coffers of gold.
> Richer than I you can never be—
> I had a mother who read to me.

Richer, perhaps not . . . but I hope you and your kids can be at least that rich! Let's explore a few more ways you can leave a reading legacy—whether you're a parent, a teacher, a CEO, or just someone who wants to use his or her influence for lasting good.

Help Kids Learn to Love Books and Reading

In August 2005, the *Orlando Sentinel* reported that half the kids in local schools would be put through mandatory remedial reading classes. It was that bad. What caught my heart as I read this story were the words of a tenth-grade student who said, "I don't want to be here. I don't think anybody does." One of her classmates complained about the classes. "I can read," she said. "I just don't like reading."

"Let's call it an assault," said Florida Department of Education reading director Mary Laura Openshaw regarding the remedial classes. "It's a push to make sure these kids aren't left behind" (Dave Weber, *Orlando Sentinel*, August 4, 2005).

I couldn't be more pleased that our schools are eagerly trying to correct their problems. I'm also excited to see so much research being done to discover how kids learn. Hopefully, every discovery will propel our kids forward, offering them the best life possible on this planet.

Stephen Strang, founder of *Charisma* magazine, said it well in a letter to the editor in response to an article about Hazel Haley, a beloved former teacher. "She gave me a lifelong love of books," Strang wrote. "As I recall, she required me to read and report on twenty-five books my senior year. Today I'm a publisher, and I have no doubt that impressionable year in her classroom moved me toward my chosen profession" (*Orlando Sentinel*, May 22, 2006).

We can all be like Hazel Haley if we'll just model reading and love of books for our kids. In an article called "How to Raise an A+ Student" (*Reader's Digest*, September, 2006), writer William Beaman discovered one common factor in raising high-achieving children is parents who take an active interest in their children's education. "Most critical of all," the article said of one home, "there are books—hundreds and hundreds of books, lining shelves and resting on tables. Their parents began reading . . . instilling a love of books by example, not pressure."

Modeling reading is what we all need to do—but we've also got to be careful we're encouraging depth along the way. Some think it doesn't matter what we encourage kids to read, as long as they are reading. That is just not the whole truth. An article called "Literary Losers" (*Wall Street Journal*, July 7, 2006) noted this astute observation from Ellen Fader, president of the Association for Library Services to Children: "Child readers haven't cemented their tastes. Adults serve as intermediaries in introducing books to young people."

Kelly Robertson is a teacher at Northridge Middle School near Crawfordsville, Indiana, whom I met during the summer of 2006 after speaking at Student Leadership University in Orlando. I asked Robertson to share her thoughts, from a teacher's unique perspective, about why kids struggle with reading today. Her answers were both sad and challenging: "Kids have lost the joy to read," she wrote, "and many more have lost confidence in their ability to read . . . The sad truth is they will not get much help after third grade." If kids with reading problems are not identified in time, Robertson told me, they are assumed proficient by the time they land in middle school. Another problem, Robertson said, comes from parents who place greater value on sports than on reading. Now I am certainly in favor of sports as team player and bodybuilders, but please, parents, place reading first in your child's life!

Kids need to learn to make inferences and have a bigger world than many are receiving in which to relate what they read, Robertson continued. Vocabularies need building, along with the ability to find the main idea in what is being read.

Additionally, Robertson offered her own list of great books about reading. With her permission, I've included that list as a resource in the back of this book. Parents and teachers, I beg you to do what it takes to make reading enjoyable for your kids!

I remember what it was like to have tough-loving parents and teachers who doled out assignments with the option, "Do it, or else." All of us kids knew what that meant, and while we dreaded those chores, we grew up to be better people because of them. I'm not necessarily knocking "forcing" kids to do things they don't want to do—sometimes, we must—but it breaks my heart to hear these kids say they don't like to read. I love to read! Why can't we help America's kids learn to love it, too?

Children are made readers on the laps of their parents.

—Emilie Buchwald, author

Not long ago, I received an e-mail from a young lady who had been in attendance at one of my talks. As usual, I'd presented my reading challenge. Paula wrote, "Thank you . . . for such an inspiring presentation. I have decided to give myself the hour a day and devote it to reading." I'd like you to notice two things in what Paula said: 1) she recognized that taking up my challenge was a gift to herself, and 2) she'd been inspired by what I said. Folks, I know I'm not the only person who thinks this message is critically important. You can inspire someone to read just as well as I can. Just do it.

Oprah Winfrey tells a story of her childhood that grieves my soul. As a young girl, Oprah recalls, she was made to feel "as though something was wrong with me because I wanted to read all the time." She remembers her mother's anger and her hot words when, while tearing a book out of young Oprah's hands, she reprimanded her. "You're nothing but a something-something bookworm," one writer recorded Oprah's mother saying. "And I'm not taking you to no library." Imagine the pain these words must have caused this young girl. Books became not only Oprah's friends, but "sometimes her only friends. And, she says, they made her who she is today" (Marilyn Johnson, *Life* magazine, September 1997).

Mom, Dad . . . wouldn't you like to know you're raising an Oprah Winfrey? Encourage your kids to read, and make it fun— any way you can. Help them to see that books are their friends, for life.

Venus and Mars

Not long ago, a *Newsweek* article noted the difference between the way boys and girls learn, citing new findings that there are actual differences in male and female brains. I don't recall being interviewed for this article, but I could have saved them some time. With my eleven boys and eight girls, believe me, I've known that for years!

Posing the question, "Are separate classrooms the best way

to teach kids?" *Newsweek*'s Peg Tyre offered a profile of some controversial ideas floating around the education world. One theory, actually being practiced in a few schools, is based on research that shows boys learn differently from girls. (Really? I'm amazed!) In order to level the playing field, some administrators are selecting curriculum based on these learning preferences and actually dividing classes by gender. Seventy percent of children diagnosed with learning disabilities are male. Most boys, in fact, struggle in school. Those facts stunned me, but that wasn't all. "Eighty percent of high-school dropouts are boys," she wrote, "and less than forty-five percent of students enrolled in college are young men."

Whether or not we need to have separate classrooms is an argument I'll leave to educators, but one thing is clear—all of us who care about children need to invest in these young lives. No matter what your educational philosophy, every kid I've ever known, especially the precious lives that have become part of my family, responds positively to one thing: love. If we love our kids, we need to do more than just pat them on the head and send them off into adulthood. Spend time with them; do what you can to understand them, tough as that can often be. Let them know you're on their side.

From your parents you learn
love and laughter and how to put one foot
before the other. But when books are
opened you discover that
you have wings.

—Helen Hayes, actress

There's a verse from the book of Proverbs that's often quoted with regard to raising our kids. I like how the Amplified Version puts it: "Train up a child in the way he should go [and in keeping with his individual gift or bent], and when he is old he will not depart from it." Study that child you love. Watch what he or she is naturally drawn to. Help him develop his natural skills. Show her how to strengthen her gifts.

One way to do that is by being a role model. Nothing has frustrated me more in recent years than to hear a few top athletes and other prominent individuals deny that kids look up to them. We are all influencers—all of us! Everywhere, every day, some young life is watching us. Make sure you are an influence for good.

Encourage all those young brains, male or female, to enjoy curling up with a good book. No matter how our brains learn, we can all learn to love books. We can all be richer for reading.

In the School

High-school English teacher Patrick Welsh, writing in the August 4, 2005, edition of *USA Today*, bemoaned the fact that in an age when students are reading less and text messaging more, teachers "saddle students with textbooks that would turn off even the most passionate reader." Welsh advocates dumping current "megatextbooks" that offer thin overviews of a variety of topics and brief snippets of classics, watering down real education, in favor of "the kinds of books that will make kids want to do sustained reading, to get lost in the written word. For English classes, that's paperback novels (whole novels) and collections of short stories (complete short stories) and poetry." Welsh may be on to something. Teachers and educators, I urge you to consider the future of our children, not just those works that please textbook publishers.

In my hometown of Orlando during the summer of 2005, Grand Avenue Elementary School conducted a three-week literacy program to get kids reading. For three hours each morning, the kids would read, write, sing songs, and play. Making work fun seems to have paid off. "It's fun, it's exciting, and they almost don't even realize they're learning," said kindergarten teacher Amy Mizell (*Orlando Sentinel*, July 30, 2005).

Richard Lapchick, director of the DeVos Sport Business Management Program, wrote me following a speaking engagement before his students. His letter was similar to Paula's, which I mentioned a few pages earlier. "I can assure you," he wrote, "that many of our students are now in the 'book a week' mode. I hear from students from past classes who tell me that they still do the same."

My friend Jay Strack is founder of Student Leadership University in Orlando. This organization trains thousands of young people each year in leadership skills, and Jay puts a heavy emphasis on reading as one of the critical blocks of successful leadership. During the summer I come and speak each week to a different group, occasionally dedicating the whole hour strictly to reading, sharing with the young people the same principles I've put down in this book.

A number of years back, unbeknownst to me, one young man by the name of Alex Schwyhart, from Bentonville, Arkansas, decided to take me up on my challenge to read an hour a day. When Strack was in Bentonville some years later, he paid a visit to young Alex's father, who told him, "I'm going broke on your organization!"

"What do you mean?" Strack said. "The fees aren't *that* much."

"No," said the father, "I'm talking about the books I've had to buy for my kid! He's read over *five hundred* of them!" Needless to say, Strack was astounded.

"Come here," said the father. "I'll show you." On their bookshelves were over five hundred books that young Alex had read over about a five-year period. Impressed, Jay called to Alex, pulled a book from the shelf, then another and another, asking Alex if he could remember anything he'd read. Sure enough, young Alex had a pretty good idea what each book was about.

Today, Alex is going on nineteen and enrolled at the London

School of Economics—the most prestigious economics school in the world—pursuing a degree in international business. He was admitted at age seventeen, the youngest American student ever enrolled. He plans to go on to Oxford, and his long-range goal is to be president of the United States.

That's what books can do in the right hands and with the right mind. Educators, I urge you to take up this mantle as well. Don't just assign reading—inspire it.

If we care about the world of tomorrow, whether you and I are here to see it or not, we need to become "Reading Renegades"— don't let trends determine our actions. Dare to be countercultural. Become a "Word Warrior." The future of our nation—and our children—is at stake.

One note of caution: should you decide on a method to motivate your students to read, remember this lesson from Harrington Park, New Jersey, school principal Scott Davies. According to an Associated Press article Davies challenged his 700 students to read 10,000 books and then let them choose their own reward. When they met his challenge earlier than anticipated, they chose to shave the school's initials (HP) into Principal Davies' hair and sent him on an overnight "campout" on the school's rooftop—with nighttime temperatures below freezing ("Cold Campout on Roof for NJ Principal," December 9, 2006). So my advice is to choose that reward yourself or be extremely careful to set parameters. But by all means, get your students reading.

In the Home

I grew up, as I've said before, in a reading family. My dad was a schoolteacher in Wilmington, Delaware; my mother was a college graduate with a great love of literature. I grew up in that environment and was probably read to in the womb. I can't remember a time when books weren't a part of my life.

*Our children are the living messages we
send into a time we shall not see.*

—Art Linkletter

Baseball was a boyhood passion of mine. When my family took occasional trips to New York City, I visited some amazing old bookstores. With money I'd saved from my paper route, I purchased a few, all related to my love of baseball. I have them to this day. Some of them were printed in the early 1900s (and I'm not *that* old!) . . . not antiques, but still valuable, and great reminders that my parents set the reading example for me.

As a dad, I made sure my kids understand that books are as important as food and daily exercise. Thanks to my parents' example, I know the atmosphere established in the home is critical in creating lifelong readers. I pray it's a lesson my kids have absorbed and will pass on to their progeny.

Dan Benson is a publisher with Cook Publications Ministries in Colorado Springs, Colorado. What influenced him to make this career choice? Here's how Dan tells it:

> From my earliest days, Mom would read to us (my three older brothers and me) in a lively, animated manner, which made story time a favorite time. Everything from Bible stories to favorite children's books. This made me eager to hold the books myself and "read" along, and eventually actually learn to read. That early, consistent start fostered a love of reading and of books, which energized my aptitude and desire to read well in school as well as for pleasure.
>
> Indirectly, though my parents never pushed me into writing, my love of books also led me, I think, to tinker with writing . . . both fiction and non. I sold my first article at age eleven, followed by several short fiction pieces in my early and mid-teens. In high school and

college, I edited and wrote for my school newspapers and moved into magazines right after college. Then I authored my first of several books at age twenty-seven (*The Total Man*, Tyndale House). It sold 200,000 copies and spoiled me. I thought they'd all sell that easily!

Mom was a Christian bookstore manager in my early school days; later in life she got her master's in literature and taught high-school English and literature. As I grew older, we often discussed the classics—what we liked and didn't like and why. We continued to do so until her final years on this planet . . . As her eyes succumbed to macular degeneration, she had at least one book-on-tape going every day, and during our phone visits we would discuss what she was "reading."

I got into book publishing in the late '70s and have been in Christian book publishing ever since, serving at Thomas Nelson, Multnomah, and WaterBrook (the Christian book division of Random House). A few years ago, I accepted the challenge to help Cook Communications Ministries (formerly David C. Cook) develop and grow its relatively new book division, and while the challenge is huge, we're now well on track to be among the major players in Christian book publishing. Time doesn't allow for much writing on the side, but I jump in occasionally and peck away at the keyboard. But . . . I'm rarely without a good book in my hand. See what you started, Mom?

Is it possible Benson's career choice was influenced by the reading home in which he grew up? I would argue that it was, and decidedly so.

Orlando Magic favorite Grant Hill recalls, "My parents were both big readers, and we always had books in every room. My mom and dad read to me as a child, and I've been a reader ever since. It's a wonderful experience to get lost in a book. It can be fiction or books about money, sports, or self-help. Tamia and I have books for our daughter. She'd rather hear a story than go out and play. She has a curiosity about her and enjoys learning, growing, and evolving."

*I look back now with amazement at the small
accidents that put certain books before me, and
how in my childhood I was taken up by books, as
if by the strong arms of a parent I'd never known
and had been badly missing, to be carried inside
to the warm safe place of reading.*

—Vince Passaro, author, in
0, The Oprah Magazine (July 2006)

"My mother adored books, viewing them as a source of great enjoyment, rather than a chore or tool," said Rudy Giuliani, former mayor of New York.

She planted the idea that a book could take a reader anywhere; that anything could be mastered, if one read deeply enough. She used to tell me that reading a book could take you on a vacation. She went to the Pacific Islands reading James Michener's *Hawaii* and visited Tuscany by reading Irving Stone's fictionalized biography of Michelangelo, *The Agony and the Ecstasy*.

I couldn't wait to take a history course in school. When I did, I treasured my textbooks, and would touch and smell them, fascinated with the worlds depicted inside. I still like the look, feel, and smell of books.

In my early days of schooling, I hewed to my mother's strict schedule of homework first and play later. As I grew older and discovered baseball and girls, I naturally resisted that discipline, but even as I found excuses to put off studying and would resort to cramming, just before exams, the love of learning was still there. Sure, there were certain subjects that bored me and other academic chores I didn't relish, but, by and large, my mother created a great love of acquiring knowledge . . . an excitement about learning new things.

---

*One way to educate the next generation
is to read to them. I'll leave my kids a
legacy of over 10,000 volumes.*

—Rick Warren, author and pastor

If you have young children in your home, read out loud to them. Initially, they may not think you're as exciting as Game Boy or SpongeBob SquarePants, but those kids will love the time you spend with them, and they'll pick up on your positive reading cues. I really can't urge you strongly enough to consider the priceless value of reading aloud to children.

Making reading interactive is a key to keeping it alive in our culture. First Lady Laura Bush says, "One of the really great things about a book club or about going to a literature class is reading books that are hard. You get a lot more out of them when you read and discuss them."

She's so right! If all we read are books that are easy to understand, we limit our potential. Discussing books with other readers helps you see more deeply into their truths.

I was encouraged to read in *USA Today* (May 8, 2006) an article about the development in communities across America of parent/children reading groups, like the mother/daughter book group at the Webster Place Barnes & Noble in Chicago, the public library pajama party nights in Yorba Linda, California, and the parent/child book groups begun by Wall Street traders turned writers Nancy and Larry Goldstone. What an amazing bonding concept! I applaud every adult involved and encourage others to do likewise. All it takes to make a difference like this is a heart to step out and do it. All our lives can be so much richer for investing them in children—and so much poorer for the absence of a child's presence.

> *I read for one reason: because my father*
> *had read to me. And because he'd read to me,*
> *when my time came I knew intuitively*
> *there is a torch that is supposed to be passed*
> *from one generation to the next.*
>
> —Jim Trelease,
> *The Read-Aloud Handbook*

Reading may not be the most social activity you could choose, but reading makes each of us more interesting to be with socially. I believe we all need time with those special friends we can only find in books. I believe this so firmly that I continue to give books to my kids, even though they're grown. Finally, one summer, my son Bobby, who manages a minor-league team for the Washington Nationals, couldn't take it anymore. "Dad," he pleaded with me on the phone, "please . . . no more books! I don't have a way to get them home."

Inside Edition anchor Deborah Norville told *Woman's Day* (July 11, 2006), "Every study I've seen says kids who see their parents read become more committed readers themselves. But most of us are so busy that the only time we read is late at night when our children don't see us." To make sure that does not happen in her home, Norville said, she and her husband are selective in making commitments outside the home. They understand that the more time you spend with your kids, the more likely they are to see you reading.

Though I don't have the reference, I recall reading a piece written by Margaret Thatcher in which she remembered that her father, Alfred Roberts, was a passionate reader. He would take his young daughter regularly to the library to check out two books— one fiction and the other a nonfiction history, biography, or other serious work. Each book had to be thoroughly read and discussed before returning it the next week. Her father understood how to shape young minds.

During a recent visit with Chris Goulard, pastor of stewardship with a church in Southern California, one of the items on his wall grabbed my attention. Written in pencil on lined tablet paper, I read the words: "Top Ten Reasons Why I Love My Dad!" Young Milton Goulard's number-one reason: "He reads books to us." Clearly, this dad knows how to steward his kids in the right direction. Dare to be like that!

That's what it comes down to, folks. Kids remember the focused time you spend with them—and they love it most when you read them books.

Be a Reading Hero

As I've said, my mom was a huge influence on my life. Because of her example, my household has been filled with books and readers. My wife, Ruth, and I read voraciously, and each one of our nineteen kids has seen how we value reading.

What do your kids see you doing regularly? Do you read? Are books your favorite pastime? If they aren't, I hope this book is giving you serious thoughts about giving them new status in your life.

Former first lady Barbara Bush expressed a pretty strong opinion regarding what she thinks most of us *don't* do when she said, "I'll bet you half the Americans out there have never read a book for fun." She also stressed the importance of setting the example in the home. "Kids who don't see their parents reading are less likely to do so themselves."

While speaking in Philadelphia early in November 2006, I saw an article in the *Philadelphia Inquirer* in which Senator Barak Obama (Illinois) said, "Parents should work early with their kids to get them started reading . . . If we can get our young people entering school knowing the alphabet and understanding the concept of reading, that makes an enormous difference." I especially appreciated Obama's suggestion that communities encourage local volunteer organizations to develop programs for reading aloud to children whose parents are not available or able to read to them. Kids need to know reading matters to the adults in their lives. If it can't be Mom and Dad, it needs to be someone.

Through his popular book, *The Read-Aloud Handbook*, author and reading instructor Jim Trelease reveals that he knows what it means to get a head start in life. If more of us knew his secret, and why it's so powerful, we might one day be able to eliminate government-sponsored reading programs. It's not that those programs aren't worthwhile, but if we all valued reading and emphasized reading in our homes, those tax dollars wouldn't be needed in this arena. Here's the key discovery: kids who are read to regularly from their earliest days become better readers. Kids who are read to in the home are ready, eager readers by the time school comes along.

Trelease cites the story of a little boy whose mother began reading to him almost the moment he was born. Poems, picture books, stories, novels—whatever he would sit still for. He learned to love the sound of words. By age four, the boy had taught himself to read, and by the time he entered school, he was ready for advanced programs. Not every child who is read to early in life will do likewise, but every child who is read to will have a head start on life.

There's nothing more delicious than
reading to your kids, and later,
when they're older, being read to by them.

—Deborah Norville, *Woman's Day* interview (July 2006)

Giving children the gift of books and a love for reading is without a doubt one of the greatest treasures we can bestow upon them. We owe it to them, and to ourselves! And what's more, we can do that right now. It's not something we have to leave in a last will and testament, not something that needs to be argued over in probate courts or placed in a trust. We just need to set the example by reading, and by reading to our kids. Knowing how to read and loving it puts kids ahead of their classmates and makes them far less likely to make poor choices along the path to adulthood.

"If we can read and write, we can learn. If we can learn, we can get a job, and support ourselves and our families," continued Barbara Bush. "We'd be less tempted to turn to drugs, alcohol, or crime, or to drop out of school, or get pregnant before we're ready. We'll have pride and be able to enjoy the very best in life . . . including a good book of bedtime stories with our children."

Who doesn't want a future like that? You can have it—no matter what age you are right now—if you'll model reading before others . . . especially children.

I have a passion to learn that's driven me all my life. Here I am now, in my midsixties, and the desire is intensifying on a daily basis. The expression, "so many books, so little time," has true meaning for me. Several years ago, I passed on receiving a salary increase with the Magic and took a monthly book stipend instead. And I'm a man with nineteen kids! I've never regretted that decision.

The best investment you can make is in your ongoing education, and reading is the best method in the world to keep your brain active, alert, and on fire.

The *Beyond* Factor:
So What Can I Do About It?

Are you getting the message? The future—not just yours, but everyone's—is up to you! Each person is accountable to every other person in some way and at some time. Right now, please make these decisions:

1. **See others as your partners in time.** When you begin to realize that other people around you are your contemporaries, part of the same "era in history," it can dramatically alter your attitude toward them. Remember John Donne's words, "no man is an island," and be involved in all mankind. On its surface, that may sound like a task too huge for any one person, but books offer that connection. They are like time machines, allowing us to move backward and forward at will.

2. **Be a reading promoter.** Make yourself aware of all the opportunities around you to read, to encourage reading, and to promote reading in the lives of others. Find out what your schools are doing today to change tomorrow through books. Then through the moments of your life, whether you're at work, at school, or at home, find time to talk about books. It's clear that people need to think about books more. Why should it all be up to Oprah and Pat? You can deliver this message, too.

3. **Be a read-aloud reader and a reading role model to some child in your life.** Think it doesn't matter? Consider these words from basketball star Chris Webber, who named his mother as the number-one reading influence in his life. "She was a teacher. Even before the NBA, she had me working at her school with her students, or day care, with reading projects. Just growing up in our house, reading was something that was important. We had to read for an hour to watch TV, to play outside. When you have to read, you're going to do it, and you'll find a way to like it in the end.

   "As I got older, I realized what a huge impact reading had on my life. When you go through troubling times, you tend to look for guidance; you tend to look for someone who has had your same problems. Some of my favorite books have been about people's different struggles. I enjoy reading autobiographies, to see that everybody goes through their own trials, tribulations, *and* triumphs. Autobiographical books have really been great to me."

It's amazing, once you realize how completely false the notion is, that so many of us think we're alone. "No one has ever had my problems!" we often wail. Yes, they have! You have not been singled out to be snakebit! Books are one awesome way to discover that connection, to find a friend or two who's been where you are, who's hurt like you're hurting.

Kids need to know a) that reading matters, b) that it matters to you, and c) that books hold the key to life's answers. You can help them make that discovery.

Whether it's in the home or out in public, determine to show other people that books matter to you. Make yourself this promise, "I'll read to the kids in my life or seek out opportunities to read to kids through school programs, library programs, radio programs, or any other way I can. My goal, starting today, is to get young hearts excited about books." You won't regret it—but you might if you don't do it!

4. **Take time every day to consider your own story.** Study the pattern of your life, look for the dramatic moments, the tragedies, the bright spots, the lessons. What part are you playing in the big picture? Make it your aim to seek out the answer, and take responsibility for shaping your future.

5. **Get to know your story in such a way that you can share it at any moment.** Have open ears and an open heart for the one who needs to hear it most. Write it down and condense it into a sentence—the theme of your life. Each of us has one.

Early in their *Toy Story* relationship, cowboy Woody watched Buzz Lightyear's antics and remarked, "That's not flying! That's falling—with style." Your initial attempts at launching your personal vision may feel like that. But if you never try, how will you ever know if you can reach infinity—*or beyond.*

Read for Your Life Way No. 11:

Keep It Going—The *Final* Factor

19

Hope Is in Sight

An April 2003 *Reader's Digest* story told of an airport customer-service agent approached by a frantic woman. *She must have missed her flight,* he thought, and was surprised when she shrieked, "I left my book on the plane!" He asked the book's title, expecting it to be a rare volume, and had to suppress the laughter when she answered, somewhat hysterically, *"Don't Sweat the Small Stuff."*

Reading never fails to enrich our lives, but ultimately its primary value is realized through application. Like that woman at the airport, if we don't use it . . . we'll lose it!

What can you and I do to solve our reading dilemma?

In "The Closing of the American Book," the op-ed by author Andrew Solomon cited in our first chapter, Solomon says, "While there is much work to be done in the public schools, society at large also has a job. We need to make reading, which is in its essence a solitary endeavor, a social one as well, to encourage that great thrill of finding kinship in shared experiences of books. We must weave reading back into the very fabric of the culture, and make it a mainstay of community."

Folks, I hope by now you're getting the message. We can DO this! Reading itself may be a solitary occupation, but it requires a united effort to keep it large in our culture, and reading needs to be huge. Books must eclipse all competitors for our time and attention. This is essential to our survival.

Get Involved

For all the bad news and sad statistics, there is hope—great hope! In addition to adults like you and me who are taking my reading challenge, organizations are backing reading programs, and groups are encouraging both kids and adults to read more. I mentioned just a few of them in Chapter 13, like Read to Achieve and Reading Is Fundamental.

People like Oprah Winfrey, with her multimillion-viewer audience, are hosting reading groups. Oprah's Book Club has become the coveted venue, not only of her viewers (primarily women), but even of writers and publishers. They're vying to make Oprah's list! I'm all for competition, but the important thing is that people are reading—and loving every word.

---

*To be well-informed, one must read
quickly a great number of merely instructive
books. To be cultivated, one must read slowly and
with a lingering appreciation the comparatively
few books that have been written by men who
lived, thought, and felt with style.*

—Aldous Huxley

Oprah has even mastered a way to make reading a social networking event. Through her book clubs, people are meeting in small groups all over the nation to discuss the hidden meanings in classic novels, the sage wisdom in self-help books, the uncovered treasures in history books.

An article in *BusinessWeek* (October 10, 2005) commented on Oprah's ability to "open readers' wallets." Writer Hardy Green opined that Oprah succeeds because she provides the "guidance and sense of community bookstores no longer provide." As we mentioned a few pages ago, bookstores are beginning to reclaim and renew their role as a community gathering place. But Green makes a good point, and one bookstore owners would do well to heed.

"It all boils down to the difficulty many people have in discovering a new read," Green wrote. While there are plenty of places to read book reviews and get recommendations, there's something about Oprah's approach that works. It's called "the personal touch." No matter how much we rave about Wal-Mart and online shopping, we all long for that personal touch from someone else. And, I believe, we desperately need it.

So if you love reading, why not be like Oprah? Why not meet with the bookstore owner in your town and propose an Oprah night . . . only you'll be Oprah. Whether it's once a quarter, once a month, or once a week, host an informal evening of book reviews. Maybe tie it to those book-signing events. You writers out there, why not promote reading by putting on an event like this? It can only help your own future book sales.

Hope for Greater Literacy

On the old Jack Benny radio program, the comedian frequently teased bandleader Phil Harris for being illiterate. In one particular episode, Benny said, "Phil, you can't even write your own name. What do you do when you have to write somebody a check?" Harris replied, "Same as you. I take a shot of Novocain."

Fifty years ago, humor like this was funny because, thanks to education, illiteracy was becoming rare. Today, it's no laughing matter. But there is great hope for those who still struggle with reading issues.

Earlier in this book, we cited alarming statistics regarding illiteracy—not just around the world, where at least half the population is illiterate, but right here in the United States, where, according to one *USA Today* article (December 16, 2005), one out of every twenty adults has below basic reading skills. With the right understanding, we can turn those numbers around. If you and I simply care enough about what the future holds, illiteracy can be wiped out. There's no good reason this can't be done. Illiteracy is not fun.

Masters champion George Archer, who died in September 2005, kept a secret all his life. With a golf club he was hard to beat, but hand him a book or a pen, and it was a different story. George Archer was illiterate. His widow, Donna, told *Golf for Women* magazine that her husband worried about going back to the Masters to defend his title. "He was afraid fans would want him to personalize the autographs he signed or that he'd have to read some prepared sentences on television."

In February 2006, *PARADE* ran a stunning story about Jacques Demers, the man who led his Montreal Canadiens to the Stanley Cup in 1993. A nearly impossible home life growing up caused young Jacques to live most of his days in hiding, pretending everything was okay. Survival became his only escape route, and he did what he had to do. That path did not include excelling in school. When he managed to land a nearly miraculous opportunity in professional hockey, he put his survival skills to work by getting others to do the paperwork for him. No one ever caught on.

In spite of his successes, the shame of not being able to read haunted Demers. He thought it meant he was "dumb." Through professional help, he learned nothing could be further from the truth. Demers finally came out and told his story. He's talking about it now, and he's learning how to read, slowly. "I don't have to lie anymore," Demers told a *New York Times* interviewer. And I can only imagine what his life must have been like all those years! In the same interview, Philip Fernandez of Frontier College, Canada's oldest literacy organization, said, "people who are illiterate feel shame. If you are illiterate, you really have to use your brains, because you are always trying to fake it."

After years of counting on others to read for her, years of "fudging" the facts and hiding her inability to read, Rosa McDonald finally realized she needed help. According to a story in the December 3, 2005, *Orlando Sentinel*, it was thanks to friends who cared enough to tell her she'd never succeed without basic reading skills that McDonald finally picked up the phone and called Orlando's Adult Literacy League.

Florida's Orange County jail boasts a program called the Literature 'n Living book club, aimed at expanding the world of the troubled youths who frequently spend time in their jail cells. Participants are required to read a book, pass a test on it, and make a speech about it, in return for a brief visit home. "Hopefully," program founder John Richter told the *Orlando Sentinel* (November 6, 2005), "we'll get these kids to read sentences instead of serving them." Who doesn't want hope like that?

Admitting we need help is hard! No one is saying solving this problem is easy. But it is solvable. Don't accept defeat!

Read the Signs

Not long ago, I read about a girl named Danielle who read 700 books. Because her elementary school was involved in a program sponsored by Target stores, Danielle had been motivated early in the school year to set a lofty reading goal for herself—one that included reading ten books *a night*! That wipes me out completely. She won a medal for her achievement, but I know in the long run, she won far more. Danielle and other children like her win a lifetime of rewards from reading—rewards that result in empowered lives.

Many businesses sponsor programs to encourage reading. I applaud that! It's great when I am on the road to see phrases like, "The more you read . . . the better you get!" and "The only way to get better at reading is to do it" on signs everywhere I go. I've mentioned the NBA's Read to Achieve program. As a basketball professional, nothing pleases me more than to see my own chosen peer group involved in promoting reading. But the NBA is just one of many organizations that understand what the final score will be for those who lack reading skills—and who are proactively doing something to turn that future around.

Reading First, signed into life by President George W. Bush in 2002, is a nationally recognized program aimed at empowering all children to become successful early readers. In my home state of Florida, former governor Jeb Bush said, "Being a successful reader is the first building block to lifelong learning." During the promotion for the Disney/Walden film *The Chronicles of Narnia: The Lion, the Witch and the Wardrobe*, released in December 2005, Governor Bush, as part of the "Just Read, Florida!" initiative he sponsored beginning in 2001, actively encouraged Florida schoolchildren to read the book on which the film was based, written by C. S. Lewis.

A story from Associated Press's Carl Hartman ("National Endowment for Arts Urges Reading"), dated March 24, 2006, noted the theme of our Ray Bradbury novel with a government that "forbids people to read books," and happily contrasts it with our own. "Today's U.S. government," Hartman reports, "urgently wants people to read books, not burn them!" He cites a program called "The Big Read," in which a community selects a single book to read and discuss in a monthlong event. "Industries and governors have complained that Americans are reading less just when today's jobs call for people who can read better. The National Endowment for the Arts, which organized the Big Read projects, believes that people who read more will make better citizens."

In addition to reading programs, tools like Hooked on Phonics have become popular and more affordable as time goes on. Smart software companies are rushing to meet the need for reading tools, too.

Movies, of course, should never take the place of books, but they are a perfect vehicle for encouraging reading. It takes great stories for great movies to happen, and most of those stories are originally found in a book somewhere. Want to know more? Read the book!

Every book is an action,
and every great action is a book.

—Martin Luther

It's great to see our leaders—whether in politics or sports or business—getting actively behind reading programs. But the most important single factor in raising reading levels and improving reading scores is you. You are the only person who can influence others with those passions and skills that are uniquely yours. Did you know that you are a leader? You are. Even if you're not a movie or sports star, someone is watching you. People in your life are influenced by you. The things you do and the choices you make impact them in ways you may never fully know. "Leadership," said Rick Warren, "is influence." Every day you are influencing others—either for good or for bad.

New Trends in Learning

Ben Feller, writing in November 2005 for the Associated Press, reported on an innovative program being welcomed into schools throughout America that involves reading to dogs. That's right, trained therapy canines are helping kids become doggone good readers. "Every Tuesday at Washington Grove Elementary," Feller wrote, "students who struggle with reading get a private session with Ross, an Irish setter, or with Tucker, a golden retriever . . .

"The READ teams—Reading Education Assistance Dogs—are redefining teachers' pets across the country. The dogs and their handlers . . . help children overcome their fear of mistakes."

A small piece in *Newsweek* echoed this trend when it reported on schools in New York, New Jersey, and across the nation tapping in to the power of reading to dogs ("A Reader's Best Friend," December 11, 2006). It may sound a little radical, but if it works, why not?

I'm thrilled to see so many new ideas coming along to make reading as fun for kids as it ought to be. There is so much competing for their attention today. It's up to us adults to steer them toward the right choices—activities that grow them up into productive, contributing world citizens.

Chris Whittle, CEO of privately operated Edison Schools, has authored a book called *Crash Course*, in which he outlines ideas for a total school makeover. He challenges traditional ideas about public education—ideas that result in bored readers, among other problems. Whittle suggests involving kids more in their own education. Maybe it's time for ideas like this. "[B]y high school," Whittle writes, "imagine that only one-third of a student's time was in a traditional classroom setting . . . What . . . are they doing? . . . More often than not, they will be reading! (Educators believe deeply that students should be reading, but how much of the school day do we actually allow them to do that? We say they should read in the evening, but realistically, after a long day at school and with other homework and important activities, do we really believe they can or will?) They will also be working with a small group of other students. And they might be on their computers, writing, researching, exploring, mining that almost endless, great new ethereal library, the Internet" (*Time*, August 29, 2005).

In May 2006, a few encouraging headlines popped into the news, like this one in the *Orlando Sentinel*, "A Glimmer of Hope Dawns at Ivey Lane." The story reported that recent FCAT scores reveal the formerly struggling school is slowly climbing out of the pit. All this happened, the article said, because of a new principal who ensured a teaching staff ready to deliver on the school's curriculum. The article went on to report a general improvement in FCAT scores across the state. If one corner of America can do that, imagine what can happen across the nation, when we all open up our books.

Low-Tech Books in a High-Tech World

Another encouraging sign shouts from today's business headlines, announcing partnerships between the electronic age and books. Search engines like Google.com and online retailers like Amazon.com are making it easier than ever to find exactly what you need in a book. Do you want to examine a book before you buy it? Try Amazon's "Look Inside the Book" feature. Are you doing research and need to find specific reference material? Google's engineers have been working with the University of Michigan to make UM's library available online.

According to an article in the *New York Times* magazine ("Scan This Book," May 14, 2006), "Corporations and libraries around the world are now scanning about a million books per year . . . 'This is our chance to one-up the Greeks!'" archivist Brewster Kahle told Kevin Kelly of *Wired*, who authored the *Times* article. "It is really possible with the technology of today, not tomorrow. We can provide all the works of humankind to all the people of the world."

If you've ever used the "find" tool in Microsoft Word or your Internet browser, you already know what an amazing friend it is. Technology doesn't need to spell the end of reading. Instead it can make reading more powerful than ever before. That's exciting news!

---

*Some of us have thousands of books at home,
can walk to wonderful big-box bookstores and
well-stocked libraries and can get Amazon.com to
deliver next day. The most dramatic effect of
digital libraries will be not on us, the well-booked,
but on the billions of people worldwide who
are underserved by ordinary paper books.*

—Bill McCoy, general manager,
Adobe's e-publishing business
(*New York Times*, May 14, 2006)

In a special report on books published by *Forbes* magazine
(December 1, 2006), it was reported that fears for what would
become of books due to the Internet and the rise in technology
have turned out to be unfounded. "The Internet is fueling literacy. Giving books away online increases off-line readership . . .
People still burn books. But that only means that books are still
dangerous enough to destroy. And if people want to destroy
them, they are valuable enough that they will endure." By the way,
I was encouraged to learn in this *Forbes* report that there is an
actual think tank called the Institute for the Future of the Book
("The Networked Book," Ben Vershbow; "Stop Worrying About
Copyrights," Jonathan Enfield).

Whenever you or I read a book, something very special occurs:
we are changed by what we read. Close that book, and you are not
the same person anymore. Because of what you just read, your
worldview—your understanding, your compassion for others,
your ability to engage intelligently with others—has expanded a
little. Books help us grow, and I'm not talking about standing on
them to make you look taller!

Hope in the Headlines

Greater than all the disturbing survey results are the stories of human greatness, of people reaching beyond themselves to make a better world. In 2005, Premier Radio in England sponsored "Grab a Grand, Lend a Hand" during National Giving Week. They gave away £1,000 (nearly $2,000) a day to the charity of the winning listener's choice. When Dorcas Ellu, a nurse living in Surrey, England, won the jackpot, she thought of a story she'd recently read about Watoto Childcare Ministries in Uganda. They were educating orphaned children in Kampala and desperately needed books. Dorcas's heart was touched by this need, and now, thanks to Premier Radio, she had an opportunity to help. Her winnings went to purchase books for the Watoto program.

When young Marissa Meyer of Laguna Beach needed a community project for her bat mitzvah (a young Jewish woman's coming-of-age ceremony, held at age thirteen), her love of books motivated her actions. Inspired by a lifetime of books in her home and by her mother's involvement in a shelter for battered women, Marissa got the idea to put books in those shelters for the kids who were there. In order to get product, she wrote letters to people who regularly donate to charities. When the response to her letter netted $6,000 in donations, Marissa was hooked. One library would simply not do. In the few years since that initial effort, Marissa has raised enough money to create at least nine Marissa's Libraries, from Orange County, California, all the way to Israel (*Orange County Register*, March 31, 2005).

Stories like that give me great hope for tomorrow. Combine the enthusiasm and compassion of young people like Marissa with the power of initiatives like the one recently announced by First Lady Laura Bush to combat global illiteracy, and the outlook for the future is bright indeed.

Hope at Any Age

We've talked a lot about children in this book—about instilling a love of reading early on, about influencing young lives, about reading to kids and getting them into good reading programs. But reading is for everyone, and the good news is it's never too late to pick up this hobby. It's certainly less expensive than most, and it doesn't require any special equipment.

---

*The man who has ceased to learn
ought not to be allowed to wander around
loose in these dangerous days.*

—M. M. Coady, twentieth-century
Canadian priest and educator

Evidence is emerging daily that reading keeps our brain cells going. Tamara Quintana, director of the employee-wellness program for GuideStone Financial Resources of the Southern Baptist Convention, wrote, "While there are no clear answers, there is good evidence we can delay or even prevent age-related memory loss and lessen the effect of Alzheimer's." Now, I don't know about you, but that statement gets my attention! Among the activities Quintana suggested toward this end are those that stimulate the mind, like crossword puzzles, mind puzzle games, and *reading.* "Other research suggests that the more formal education a person has, the better his or her memory and mental function are even when plaques associated with Alzheimer's are present in the brain." Now, where did I leave that Florida State course catalog?

Dr. Bernadine Healy, in the article cited earlier from *U.S. News & World Report,* wrote about research going on that's discovering the looming effects of an idle brain on future health. Minds that meander get soft and flabby. At the other extreme are brains too singularly focused, not allowing anything else in. "Though it's too early to write a prescription," she commented, "keeping the wandering brain under control is at least good food for thought." Books offer a healthy mental focus. We can become absorbed in our reading while leaving our peripheral vision available for necessary distractions.

Just as food nourishes our bodies and fuels them for exercise, so reading feeds our brains. Then when we apply what we've read, we bring the process full circle.

Books like *The Power Years,* by Ken Dychtwald (Wiley, 2005) challenge emerging baby boomers, who feel they are hitting their stride and colliding with the senior citizens' menus, to give back some of what they've been given. Imagine that!

Singer Neil Diamond is living proof that learning goes on, even after we've hit what we thought were the heights in our lives. According to one biographer, when Diamond took a hiatus from singing, he went after the college education he'd never finished and, in the process, became "an avid bookworm." When he took time off from his career, he finally found time for all the books he'd wanted to read, even studying music theory toward his goal of one day writing symphonies.

Old minds are like old horses: you must exercise them if you wish to keep them in working order.

—John Adams, U.S. president

Don't let a lack of time keep you from pursuing your dreams. If you're over forty, take my reading challenge, try it out yourself for a while, and then pass it on to someone else as quickly as you can—while you can still see them!

Seriously, friends, my goal here is to help you see there is no age limit on reading. No one will check your ID or ask for an insurance card when you order a book from Amazon or purchase a few at Borders. No Social Security cards or Medicare proof needed. You may need your glasses checked every couple of years, but that's about as tough as it gets.

There's even more good news from the publishing industry for those of us with more years behind than ahead. An article in the *New York Times* (August 12, 2004) reported that at least two major publishers, recognizing the need to reach the baby-boomer market, "have begun issuing new paperbacks by some of their most popular authors in a bigger size that allows larger type and more space between lines." To keep the books from being "too fat," they are simply making them taller. So you see? You may not even need the glasses—just room for a few tall books in your briefcase. In fact, if it catches on, this trend could give the phrase "tall tales" a whole new meaning.

Hope at Any Stage

Are you frustrated at the lack of education in your life? It's not too late! Books can offer you a rich, fully rounded education . . . no matter what you've missed out on up to now.

Pulitzer Prize–winning author William Faulkner never even graduated from high school. Do you believe that? It's true! He educated himself through reading, and he invested that time wisely on classic works like *Moby Dick, Madame Bovary*, works of Dostoevsky, and the Old Testament. Elsewhere in this book we've pointed out the struggles Winston Churchill faced in school. I wouldn't exactly call Churchill education-deficient, would you? He well understood the power of books. Charles Darwin was a poor student, also. He made up for what school couldn't offer him by reading books on everything he could find in his field.

Iron rusts from disuse; water loses its
purity from stagnation . . . even so does
inaction sap the vigor of the mind.

—Leonardo da Vinci

What I want you to know is that no matter what hand life has dealt you, from this moment on, you're in charge. If you need to improve your reading skills, the best way to do that is to pick up a book and get started. There's an old saying that goes, "Where there is life, there is hope." Are you alive? Start reading. Forget yesterday and change tomorrow, for yourself and everyone else who is blessed to know you.

In recent years, a piece originally published in England's *Punch* magazine (dated May 9, 1962) and attributed to writer R. J. Heathorn has been making the e-mail rounds. Its point is clear. It's time for what's old, tried, and true to be seen in a new light:

Introducing the new
Bio-**O**ptic **O**rganized **K**nowledge
device—trade-named: **BOOK**.

BOOK is a revolutionary breakthrough in technology: no wires, no electric circuits, no batteries, nothing to be connected or switched on. It's so easy to use, even a child can operate it.

Compact and portable, it can be used anywhere—even sitting in an armchair by the fire—yet it is powerful enough to hold as much information as a CD-ROM disc.

Here's how it works:

B.O.O.K. is constructed of sequentially numbered sheets of paper (recyclable), each capable of holding thousands of bits of information. The pages are locked together with a custom-fit device called a binder, which keeps the sheets in their correct sequence.

Opaque Paper Technology (OPT) allows manufacturers to use both sides of the sheet, doubling the information density and cutting costs. Experts are divided on the prospects for further increases in information density; for now, B.O.O.K.s with more information simply use more pages. Each sheet is scanned optically, registering information directly into your brain. A flick of the finger takes you to the next sheet.

B.O.O.K. may be taken up at any time and used merely by opening it.

B.O.O.K. never crashes or requires rebooting, though, like other devices, it can become damaged if coffee is spilled on it, and it becomes unusable if dropped too many times on a hard surface. The "browse" feature allows you to move instantly to any sheet, and move forward or backward as you wish. Many come with an "index" feature, which pinpoints the exact location of any selected information for instant retrieval.

An optional "B.O.O.K.mark" accessory allows you to open B.O.O.K. to the exact place you left it in a previous session—even if the B.O.O.K. has been closed. B.O.O.K.marks fit universal design standards; thus, a single B.O.O.K.mark can be used in B.O.O.K.s by various manufacturers. Conversely, numerous B.O.O.K.markers can be used in a single B.O.O.K. if the user wants to store numerous views at once. The number is limited only by the number of pages in the B.O.O.K. You can also make personal notes next to B.O.O.K. text entries with optional programming tools, Portable Erasable Nib Cryptic Intercommunication Language Styli (P.E.N.C.I.L.S.).

Portable, durable, and affordable, B.O.O.K. is being hailed as a precursor of a new entertainment wave. B.O.O.K.'s appeal seems so certain that thousands of content creators have committed to the platform, and investors are reportedly flocking to invest. Look for a flood of new titles soon.

found on http://www.simplysharing.com/book.htm

Throughout these pages, we've talked about the present status of reading in America and the need to bring up those numbers, to raise those scores. We've examined the many reasons for reading. I've passed on to you my tips for navigating a bookstore and shown you how to power through the pages at a faster pace. We've looked at how to leave a legacy, both by reading to kids and by writing our own stories. We've even taken a peek into the future and seen a sign or two of hope. Now let's wrap up the package. What's the bottom line of all this reading?

20

The End Result

W hat do you do with it all? What makes reading really matter to me—*and* to you? What's the end result, the upshot,
the outcome? In sports, we call it the final score. So here it is:
when you read, you LEARN!

When you learn, *you* win.

Knowledge comes, but wisdom lingers.

—Alfred Lord Tennyson

If you've ever read books or seen movies about the tragic sink-
ing of the *Titanic* in 1912, you may recall a sense of horror at the
hopelessness of the situation faced by crew and passengers, once
the "indestructible floating fortress" struck that iceberg. When I
watched the blockbuster 1999 movie, I remember feeling a sense of
betrayal at the images of those few who made it onto half-empty

lifeboats floating off to their own safety, while most of their fellow shipmates floundered, screamed for help, and ultimately drowned.

The best of all things is to learn.
Money can be lost or stolen, health and
strength may fail, but what you have committed
to your mind is yours forever.

—Louis L'Amour

If you can picture those horrific images for just a moment, think about the lifeboats. Now picture this: books are the lifeboats of our civilization. They have the power not only to change lives, but to *literally* save them. What can we do, you and I, to make sure those lifeboats are full?

Man's mind, once stretched by a new idea,
never regains its original dimensions.

—Oliver Wendell Holmes,
nineteenth-century author and physician

None of us remembers when we were infants, first relating to the world around us, but if you're a parent, or if you've watched little ones for any length of time, you can probably relate to the excitement a mom or dad feels when their child learns something new. It's chasing that look of pride and approval in our parents' eyes that keeps many of us motivated on into adulthood, to do more, expand our learning, open new vistas. We all long to hear, "Atta boy!" or "Atta girl!"

When I was just twenty-two years old, my father died tragically. We'd been very close, Dad and me. With every triumph in my life since that sad day, I've ached that he was not there with me. But somehow, when I read books and learn something new, it's as if I can see Dad's beaming face and hear his voice, saying, "Atta boy, Pat! You're doing great, son." Since I learn something new from a book almost every day, that connection with Dad keeps going, even though he's been gone more than forty years. It was Dad, after all, who got me that Pop Warner book all those years ago and set my feet on the path my life has taken.

All those years ago, my dad handed me a lifeboat. He couldn't have known where that boat would take me, but he knew enough to realize the potential destination ports were all good ones. I've heard way too many parents excuse themselves from establishing solid values in the home, from giving their kids absolutes of right and wrong, from taking their kids to church, with empty words like, "I don't want to force my views on my kids." People, listen— if we don't give our kids something to hold on to, a goal to shoot for, a home plate to slide in on—they'll drift off onto the oceans of life like boats without rudders. My dad cared enough about me to know the Pop Warner book would set high standards for my life. If we love our kids—if we love all kids and care about the future of our world—we've got to keep raising the bar!

During the summer of 2006, the *New York Times* ran a story about a revolutionary program operating in Springfield, New Jersey, aimed at turning around the lives of correctional-facility inmates by steeping them in the world of books ("Tasting Freedom's Simple Joys in the Barnes & Noble," August 2, 2006). Thanks to the efforts of people like Alison Link of Tully House, a facility operated by Community Education Centers, people whose lives had gotten turned in the wrong direction somewhere along the way are learning that books have the power to set their feet back on solid ground.

Certainly it's important for us to accept various cultural viewpoints and be willing to listen to all opinions. But why, simply to not "rock the boat," would we want to set our kids out on a raft headed for pain and disappointment, when we have it within our power to at least point them to the ship of hope?

Books are such a ship. In their pages, we find great hope! They can help set the compass heading for our lives. They can show us the top of the mountain, the high seas, and the home port.

Learning Is a Lifelong Occupation

I recall reading a story about Abe Lincoln in which he reportedly said, "Education is not given for the purpose of earning a living; it's learning what to do with a living after you earn it that counts." It's true. When we read—especially books—we gain knowledge in a few hundred pages that might otherwise take us years to learn. I know members of my gender like to think of themselves as "no directions needed," but why waste time struggling over problems someone else has solved, especially when that someone else has left you a book on the topic? Others have been there before us, so why not benefit from their perspective?

Reading gives us "knowledge of other people's knowledge of life."

—T. S. Eliot

Reading puts us in the company of the world's greatest minds and best-lived lives. Do you want to be mentored by millionaires? You may not be able to get a lunch date with legendary CEO Jack Welch, but you can read his book, *Winning* (HarperBooks, 2005). The wisdom in books like this one is worth far more than a sandwich or two. My point is, you can learn from books what you may never be able to attain otherwise. Why not read?

I agree with Rod Delmonico, head baseball coach at the University of Tennessee, who said, "You can always learn more. You can't fill your mind enough, and the best way to do that is by reading. That's a powerful method to help keep you motivated."

Our world is changing at a faster pace than ever before. NCR CEO Charles Exley underscored that fact recently when he said, "I've been in this business thirty-six years, and I've learned a lot—and most of it doesn't apply anymore."

If we're going to keep up, we've got to be reading. As noted leadership expert and author Bill Easum has pointed out, "Change itself has changed." Without reading skills—without books—we are doomed.

William Tyndale, who lived from 1494 to 1536, first translated the New Testament into English. The "church" of that era, afraid of losing its authority over people's minds, considered Tyndale's work heresy. For his efforts, they had him arrested, imprisoned, and burned at the stake in 1536. During his imprisonment, Tyndale wrote the governor-in-chief requesting several small items to make this time more bearable. Chief among his requests: "I beseech and entreat your clemency to be urgent with the Procureur that he may kindly permit me to have my Hebrew Bible, Hebrew grammar, and Hebrew Dictionary, that I may spend time with that in study."

I want you to observe two lessons from that paragraph about William Tyndale: 1) He knew that learning was a lifelong occupation, and 2) he was sacrificing his life for something many of us today, if we believe those statistics from Chapters 1 and 2, take for granted—the right to read and know and think for ourselves, rather than be told what to think and believe.

Shouldn't reading matter more to you?

You're Never Too Old–or Too Young–to Learn!

Have you ever heard the saying "you're never too old to learn"? It's easy for us to reach a place in life where we think we can just coast. We've been to school, had our career, raised our families, and now it's time to retire and "enjoy life." Sadly, far too many people arrive at that stage, only to find that within a few months of hanging up the desk plate and turning in their card keys, their health is failing. They've lost the motivation to go on. Life becomes a waiting room. We've stopped being useful and productive, so we wait for . . . for what? At a time when people are living longer than ever before in modern history, all too many of us reach the best years of our lives—the years when we have the least commitments and most opportunities—and we throw them away. But wait—aren't we supposed to be older . . . and wiser?

If we are not living our lives fully up to our last breath—if we spend our final years just as if we are waiting out the clock—may I ask, what is the point?

Believe me when I tell you, no one on Earth is ever too old to learn.

At the age of ninety-two, Supreme Court Justice Oliver Wendell Holmes, Jr., was ordered by his doctors to a brief stay in the hospital. President Franklin D. Roosevelt dropped by to visit and was surprised to find him reading from a Greek primer.

"What are you doing, Oliver?" asked Roosevelt.

"Reading," answered Holmes.

"I can see that," said FDR, "but why are you reading a Greek primer?"

Holmes answered, "Why, Mr. President, to improve my mind."

Tennis star Brad Gilbert said, "My grandfather was reading books in his eighties, and I asked him why. He said, 'There's so much I still have to learn.'"

We think of the word "mature" as meaning fully developed— and it does. But it also refers to a process. In that regard, we are all in the process of maturing. Fully developed means we've stopped. I don't know about you, but I haven't stopped. And books are one of the key elements in my maturation process.

Graydon Carter, editor of Vanity Fair, *observed of 104-year-old philanthropist and socialite Mrs. Brooke Astor, that she was always reading, two books at a time.*

—Janny Scott for the *New York Times* (August 3, 2006)

Books Offer Connectivity

That's a big word on the tech scene these days—connectivity. Computer gurus are spending countless hours making certain hardware and software talk to each other. But books have been doing this for years. Books connect us to each other today and bridge the generational divide.

Let me ask you a question: what keeps you from passing on what you know? I've observed in my life that people tend to either cling to or drift toward one of two opposite viewpoints. Either they say something like, "I already know all I need to know. Why should I teach someone else? They won't want to hear it anyhow. And besides, I need my job. Why show someone else how to do it?" Or we think, *I don't know enough to consider myself an expert in anything. Therefore, I am not qualified to teach anyone else. What would I say?*

No matter which of these two attitudes most closely describes yours, you may want to make sure you're sitting down before you read my next startling revelation. Ready? Here it is:

You will never know all there is to know! You will *never* know "enough"! Information is being added to "all" every day—at an alarming rate. We could never keep up with it. Every person ever born contributes in some way to the historical database of knowledge.

So don't get caught in either of these empty mental traps. Ultimately, they simply keep you from achieving the purpose for which you were designed.

There's one more trap that trips us up at any age. Remember the attitude that said "they won't want to hear it?" Way too many of us let ourselves become discouraged from passing on wisdom, knowledge, or advice because, when we do, we are met with arrogance that thinks it already knows, impatience that doesn't want to listen, or indifference that says, "If I'd wanted to know, I'd have asked." Because our golden treasures are not met with immediate, gushing gratitude, we think they've fallen on deaf ears or foolish hearts.

Nothing could be further from the truth.

Most of us fail to recognize wisdom when we first encounter it. It took time, after all, for *Star Wars'* Luke Skywalker to learn to trust Yoda. But what if Yoda had kept his trap shut? What if Yoda had shrugged, "The use, what is it? Never listen, he will"? In the life of every young Jedi knight comes the moment when the light saber of wisdom and truth meets the test of battle. You and I, fellow Yodas, may never see the light come on in those eyes—but it will. In time, oh, it will.

It can seem a little daunting at times, when we realize the scope of all the knowledge that's in books and compare it to the time we have to devote to reading. We can't do it all or know it all! But we can know some. So if you're still drawing breath, you can still learn from books. And that knowledge can still benefit someone else, sometime.

Books Reveal Secrets

Rudy Giuliani said, "I developed the romantic notion that one can find secret solutions in books. I intensely read about every subject I undertake, and I do so with the conviction that I will learn things about it that nobody else knows. Although I may not be able to prove it scientifically, I believe that if you read enough about something, you're going to unravel its mystery and will, ultimately, understand the fundamentals in a deeper way than simple observation would provide; then, if you have an inquiring mind, you can apply yourself to that subject and have success in ways not experienced even by those who have spent much more time on it. It doesn't always work that way, but, more often than not, a bright person who hasn't become shackled by bad habits or a 'that's the way it's always done' philosophy can be a catalyst for change."

*People could become better than
they are right now by doing one thing: reading!
This neglected activity is a pathway to greatness.
By reading, people open their minds to be
mentored by others whom they may not have the
pleasure to meet due to time and space differences.
C. S. Lewis, Socrates, and Billy Graham
are all available to talk when
I open a book to listen.*

—Sarah Neri, reading teacher at Las Palmas
Middle School in Covina, California,
from Starbucks' "The Way I See It" series #111

A bioengineer friend of mine shared some insight with me on the value of reading in his role. "A lot of people may think the books I read are boring," he told me, referring to his huge technical library, "but without them, I wouldn't know how other people have solved the problems I deal with from day to day. Books transfer knowledge, the 'how to do' part of life. Without books, that knowledge would be lost."

In his book *1776*, author David McCullough tells the story of General Nathanael Greene, a man who taught himself military tactics simply by reading about them. "It was a day and age that saw no reason why one could not learn whatever was required—learn virtually anything—by the close study of books."

In that *USA Today* interview we cited at the beginning of this book, Bob Minzesheimer asked McCullough if this is still true today. "Of course, it is. There's been a lot of nonsense written about how children and students don't like to read books and how publishers should make the print bigger or have more pictures or simplify the vocabulary. Then along came *Harry Potter* and blew all that away."

Well, I'm not sure what information is being exchanged through Harry Potter books, but McCullough's point is well taken. When we read, we learn. Whether, like Nathanael Greene, we learn how to do something, or simply open the window of our minds to understand how others think and feel, books are what make that learning possible.

Recently I engaged a young friend in a discussion about the virtues of books versus movies. Her answer pleased me. "When you're reading a book," she said, "you can pause to think about what the character is experiencing. You can't do that with movies." Unlike movies and fast-paced, commercial-interrupted television programs, books let us push the pause button on life and think awhile.

Do you want a less hurried life? Books offer a great place to find it.

Reading expands us.
It scratches those itches down deep inside.
It navigates us through virgin territory
we would not otherwise explore.

—Chuck Swindoll, author and pastor

Books Help Us Learn to
Dream Higher and Dig Deeper

Great fiction calls us out of the ordinary and stirs our hearts to noble themes. Through novels, authors often say out loud—or at least on paper—what most of us think or wonder about. We discover friends in these pages, people who think like we do, people who hurt, laugh, dream, and hope like we do. So even in works of fiction, we learn we are not alone.

By dealing with universal themes, novels help us to see ourselves as heroes on a journey through time—a journey that connects us throughout time. Even such seemingly bleak novels as Dickens's *A Tale of Two Cities* deliver a dramatic story of redemption and hope. Huck Finn understood there was something not right about the world he lived in, so he struck out for new territory in hopes of righting that wrong.

Science fiction, from Jules Verne through Ray Bradbury and beyond, lifts our minds out of the often-disturbing reality of today's headlines and helps us see what mankind *could* do, who we might become, if only we dare to go against the current.

Books may not solve all those problems that stem from human pride, passion, and possessiveness, but they show us we're not alone in this often dark, frequently lonely world.

What I'm saying, friends, is this: the right books can make the difference between a life of crime and heartache and a life fully lived, satisfying, resplendent, and fragrant.

Many of us tread a fine line between hope and despair, between throwing our lives away and investing them in making a difference. Books give us standards to shoot for, and then they raise them. Books feed our minds and nourish our souls.

Real Books Make Real Learning Faster

In this book, we've examined both current and future reading trends, and we've discussed the current wave toward electronic reading. If reading faster to read more is your goal, you might want to rethink the screen. Sun Microsystems, a major player in the technology scheme of things, conducted a survey that revealed reading from a computer screen is 25 percent *slower* than reading from paper.

It's true that these statistics will change, as it is the nature of problems to be solved over time. Already screens are being improved and web-content writers are learning to prepare copy in ways that make it easier to scan. But we're still a long way from any type of electronic reading that is as easy, convenient, or portable as the good old-fashioned book.

It's a good time to be in the book business.
The heaviest book buyers are over forty years old,
and that's the fastest-growing segment of the
population. Education is booming in America.
More Americans are earning college degrees.
And there's a post-9/11 baby boomlet that
is good for sales of children's books.

—Stephen Riggio, Barnes & Noble CEO

Even though fiction is not my personal reading choice, when it comes to reading mediums, I found myself smiling in agreement at the words of novelist Harper Lee in her letter to Oprah Winfrey (*O, The Oprah Magazine*, July 2006): "Oprah, can you imagine curling up in bed to read a computer? Weeping for Anna Karenina and being terrified by Hannibal Lecter, entering the heart of darkness with Mista Kurtz, having Holden Caulfield ring you up—

some things should happen on soft pages, not cold metal."

If learning is your goal, you'll accomplish it more efficiently by keeping a stack of books on hand—and by reading them. Save the computer for e-mail, spreadsheets, and for writing your own book.

Books Unlock Your Imagination

During a recent Christmas shopping trip, I overheard a grand-mother ask a salesclerk, "What does this toy do?" Both of them were momentarily speechless as they realized the toy was merely a role-playing device. "You mean, they'll have to pretend?" questioned the astonished grandmother. "Imagine that!"

Today's info-dominated world is full of so many "user-friendly" message options that few of us need to use our minds for much of anything anymore. Our 24/7 news culture keeps us informed to the point of even telling us what to think. Where our kids are concerned, even cartoons are no longer the slapstick sight gags that drew upon both the imagination and sense of humor, but have become overdialogued, overscripted action events that serve little purpose other than keeping them distracted so Mom and Dad can do what they want to do.

Rich Lowry, editor with *National Review*, wrote of literary chums C. S. Lewis and J. R. R. Tolkien, "[They] wanted to re-invigorate the powers of the imagination so it would be primed to detect the hints of a higher and deeper reality—'further up, further in,' as Lewis put it. A theme of the *Narnia* books is that the children instinctively knew the right thing to do because, as Lewis scholar Jonathan Rogers explains, 'they have read the right imaginative stories.'"

Don't miss that point! The children instinctively knew the right thing to do because of the stories they had read. Books have the power to inform our kids' choices—not just about what they will be when they grow up, but in their daily lives right now. And in a world where so many young people are denied the opportunity to 1) be children, and 2) grow up, shouldn't we adults want to use every tool at our disposal to give that basic human right back to them?

No longer can we afford to assume that children have read classic stories like *Alice in Wonderland, Peter Pan*, or Grimm's fairy tales. Though it was never Walt Disney's intention, the movie versions of beloved stories have largely taken their place. After all, popping a DVD into the player and parking the kids in front of the screen leaves us free to get our housework or other chores done without the little gremlins underfoot. Please, fellow parents, grandparents, teachers, and leaders—get books into these young hands, any way you can. Our very future is at stake!

The more that you read, the more things you will know. The more that you learn, the more places you'll go.

—Dr. Seuss, *Oh, the Places You'll Go!*

It's not only kids' imaginations that are sparked by books. I rarely read anything cover-to-cover without making a list of ideas that book has introduced into my mind. I dare you to try it yourself. Just see if you can read a whole book without having at least one new thought or idea.

In the business world, companies that lack creative leadership become prime targets for hostile takeovers. Do you want that same thing to happen to our nation? It could, if we continue to let the media dictate what we think. Don't get me wrong. I'm not suggesting that this "mental takeover" has a hostile intent. But it happens. Just as undeveloped bodies are ripe for disease, so lazy minds will believe what they are told.

With books feeding our minds, our imaginations develop the ability to see the higher, deeper truths to which C. S. Lewis referred. And as Walt Disney said, "If you can dream it, you can do it."

Imagine that.

Focused Learning Leads to Powerful Living

"If you've ever used a magnifying glass to concentrate sunlight on a bug or leaf," Rick Warren observed, "you've witnessed the enormous power of focused light. Nothing is more powerful than a focused life."

Author and teacher John L. Mason talks about people who stop growing, people whose goals never change, people who are standing still in life because they never grasped that power. "God's will for us," Mason writes in his book *An Enemy Called Average*, "is to grow, to continue to learn, and improve. The biggest room in our house is always the room for self-improvement.

"A famous saying reads: 'It's what you learn after you know it all that counts.' I must admit that I am somewhat of a fanatic about this. I hate to have idle time—time in which I am not learning anything. Those around me know that I must always have something to read or to write during any idle moment that might arise. In fact, I try to learn from everyone. From one I may learn what not to do, while from another, I learn what to do. Learn from the mistakes of others. You won't live long enough to make all the mistakes yourself."

I couldn't agree more, and here is where books enhance that focus—they allow us to continually learn from the mistakes of others. Books help us learn how to learn, and John Naisbitt, author of the bestselling Megatrends series of business books, says, "Learning how to learn is the most precious thing we have in life."

As you read, you'll gradually find yourself eliminating items from your reading list that don't lead you in the direction you want to go. Like road maps, you'll find yourself passing up the places you're not planning to visit. That comment comes with a warning, however. As a parent, I find myself cautioning other parents not to overlook or neglect the quiet kids when it comes to developing leadership. The same principle is true with books. Some of the most powerful, life-changing ideas come from the most understated books. Just as God-given personalities meet life influences, causing kids to grow into a variety of different leaders, the books with which we nurture our minds and souls along the way play a life-shaping role in our growth.

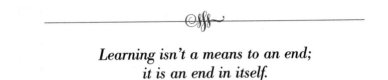

Learning isn't a means to an end;
it is an end in itself.

−Robert A. Heinlein, science-fiction author

Wal-Mart leadership guru Don Soderquist offers four ways a consistent reading plan can enhance your life (*The Wal-Mart Way*, Nelson Business, 2005):

1. "Mental exercise: It's a little harder [than watching television]. But just as physical exercise makes you stronger, reading makes you mentally sharper.

2. "Deeper levels of thinking: Books . . . can go much deeper into a topic. As you read about important subjects, you can challenge your own thinking—and grow intellectually.

3. "More interesting conversation: When you read you become a more interesting conversationalist.

4. "Spiritual development: [W]hen Gutenberg invented the printing press to produce the Bible for the common man, he forever linked the printed word with spiritual growth."

Books bring life into focus, and a focused life, like that magnifying glass concentrated on a bug or a leaf, brings fresh fire to everything it touches.

Leadership guru John C. Maxwell says we must all answer three questions in life: 1) What do we want? 2) Why do we want it? and 3) How badly do we want it?

No matter what you want from life, what you learn from books is the most direct and enriching pathway to that success. Do you hunger for accomplishment? Do you treasure wisdom? Does your heart cry out for the pain you see in this world? Do you long for influence to change it?

I urge you to diligently seek the instruction that books can speak into your life. There is no greater source of collected wisdom. It all begins with that first question, "What do you want?" If, as Solomon counsels us from the book of Proverbs, you cry out for discernment and lift up your voice for understanding, if you search for your answers as if they were hidden treasure, then you will understand.

Read, read, read. Whatever seems distant to you now is just within your grasp—let a book bring it closer.

The End Result Is Only the Beginning!

I made this point earlier, and now in our closing pages I'd like to reemphasize it: our world needs leaders! I'm not talking about power figures, dictators, or despots. By leaders, I mean servants—leaders who see the big picture, who have compassion for the needs of others, and who are willing to put their lives on the line to meet those needs.

Think about this, because it's true: each of us is a leader in some way or another because we're all influencing someone else's life. Please consider whose life you are influencing. Are you exerting a good influence? Will that person's life be better because of what they see you doing?

"Responsibility" is not a popular word these days. Too many people prefer to point the finger at others rather than shoulder blame for their own actions.

"One reason why people are unable to understand great Christian classics," wrote A. W. Tozer, "is that they are trying to understand without any intention of obeying them." He makes a great point. It's so much easier to escape accountability when we claim we don't know what it is we're accountable for. But be certain of this: that escape is only temporary. Our actions, and our inaction, will ultimately tell our life stories.

Dare to be different. Be a leader who owns up rather than talks down. "Leaders," wrote my friend Greg Morris, "are readers." Learning is the key to your growth. I fully agree with Dr. Harry L. Reeder, who has said, "Once you quit learning, you forfeit the opportunity to teach, lead, and coach others . . . The leader who intends to grow spiritually and intellectually will be on a committed course of improvement. The leader in training will read and study constantly."

"Realize," Morris adds, "that when it comes to learning you will never 'arrive'! Learning is not an event or a destination, but a lifelong process, a journey. Keep your tools sharp by exposing yourself to new ideas, new thoughts, and new technology. With the current advances in knowledge, the leader that stops will be quickly passed."

---

*I've always believed reading is an
excellent way to learn about leadership—
I always encouraged our management team at
Wal-Mart to develop their own library of good
business and personal development books.*

—Don Soderquist, former Wal-Mart
executive and leadership expert

Social writer Eric Hoffer said, "In times of change, learners inherit the Earth, while the learned find themselves beautifully equipped to deal with a world that no longer exists." Hoffer, by the way, was a man who mysteriously lost his eyesight at the age of seven and just as strangely regained it at fifteen. So distraught was he at the thought of losing it again that he set upon a campaign to read as much as he possibly could. His eyesight stayed with him for the rest of his life, and he remained a voracious reader as well as a prolific writer. In 1983, just months before his death at age eighty, Hoffer was awarded the Presidential Medal of Freedom by President Ronald Reagan. Reading rewards the reader in so many countless ways.

Be a leader in training. And recognize that your training never ends.

Biographer Doris Kearns Goodwin said of Abraham Lincoln, "He had a lifelong quest to become an educated person." May I suggest this quest as a worthy lifelong pursuit for each one of us? There's a lot of talk these days about finding our purpose in life— and we should all long to do that. I'm not sure we can fully know it without books.

When you read, you marinate your mind in the thoughts, ideas, and dreams that have made millions of hearts beat faster. When the dreams that swelled another mind to heights of grandeur connect with yours, who knows what may come of that inspiration? Walt Disney loved to tell the story of the books he read in the Kansas City Public Library during his years as a young filmmaker—a discovery that taught him all he needed to know to get started in animation. That knowledge, combined with Walt's fertile imagination, gave birth to a creative endeavor that *continues* to inspire millions of people today. Just think about that for a minute or two.

Fears of the future are put to rest when we are confident about the direction we're headed in. Books can help you set your compass headings.

Read, every day, something no one else is reading. Think, every day, something no one else is thinking. Do, every day, something no one else would be silly enough to do. It is bad for the mind to continually be part of unanimity.

—Christopher Morley, early twentieth-century writer and editor

Learning needs to be a lifelong pursuit, so I'm filled with hope when I receive letters like this one from a man who heard me speak in September 2005: "I am a typical, overworked mortgage broker who fails to find time to read. I typically read only about six books a year. After hearing your speech, I decided to read in the car for five minutes each time I park. In the two weeks since your speech, I have spent over 10.5 hours reading. Even better, my confidence has increased as a result." Now that's a dividend, my friends! That is reality speaking. And it proves that this reading thing works. Anyone can do it. I can do it. You can do it.

Throughout this book, I've presented you with facts, personal stories, and illustrations from the lives of many great, historic readers, and thoughts from influential people throughout history—all on the topic of reading. You know you need to do it. So now there is just one question that remains: are you in?

If we are imprisoned in ourselves,
books provide us with the means of escape.
If we have run too far away from ourselves,
books show us the way back.

—Holbrook Jackson, early twentieth-century
journalist, writer, and publisher

Get Ready to Change Your Life

I'd like to leave you with this story, which comes with a warning. Personal experience is a powerful teacher.

When Chuck Daly was head coach of the Orlando Magic, my wife, Ruth, and I traveled with Chuck for the NBA All-Star Weekend in New York. It involved a particularly long bus trip. I had books everywhere and read constantly. As we neared our destination, Chuck pulled me aside and said, "Pat, do you realize you haven't spoken to your wife once on this entire trip? You'd better watch it!"

I related that story to Ruth by way of apology. "Well, thank goodness for Chuck Daly!" she said. I'm so thankful that Ruth is also a reader! It makes our time together much more enjoyable, as we relax in each other's company, and in the mutual company of a good book. But I'm also a wiser man for Chuck's observing eyes and caring heart.

So here's the warning: when you decide to become a reader, you need to know that this adventure is highly addictive. TV and movie viewing will become almost agonizing time consumers as they keep you from your books. You'll be restless, full of nervous energy, eager for the moment you can dive back into the excitement of those pages. You'll hate it when the light turns green, and you have to put the book down. Reading changes your entire view of life.

With that warning, there is also this promise: you'll never regret the decision to become a reader.

If you empty your purse into your head, no one can take it away from you. An investment in knowledge always pays the best interest.

—Benjamin Franklin

Afterthoughts

W hen I set out to write this book, I began as I usually do: I asked friends and colleagues what they thought of the idea. While most agreed its time had come, one comment kept popping up: if people aren't reading, why would they want to read a book—about reading? So I realize that I may be preaching to a good many choir members out there.

But on the off chance that you are not yet a member of this vast chorus of committed readers, I hope the words, thoughts, and ideas I've shared with you here encourage you to audition. You'll be surprised to find that the choirmaster is very forgiving. He doesn't ask you to have perfect pitch, nor does he care if you can carry a tune—just be willing to join in at any time.

I hope you've come to recognize me as a man who cares deeply about your future. Perhaps someone else who cares about you—a veteran choir member, maybe—has given you this book in the hope it will drive you to become an intentional reader. If so, you are not obligated to agree. You can ignore the ideas and advice in this book, if you so choose. But why would you want to do that?

Though you and I may never have met in person, if the advice in this book has connected with your heart, then I'm sure I'll recognize you on the street. You'll be the one with the open book in your hands.

Me, too.

Throughout this book we've used excerpts from Ray Bradbury's *Fahrenheit 451*, primarily because of their obvious picture of a future world in which books and the ideas they inspire are condemned as evil. I'm not here to be an alarmist, but we have to understand the danger we are in if we continue to shrug our shoulders and plug in our video games instead of picking up books. Bradbury's main character, Guy Montag, was willing to at least ask the disturbing questions. Are you willing to do the same? If you are, there is genuine hope for the future. We can't ignore the world our kids will inherit—not if we love them. I know I do, and I believe you do, too.

A conversation I had recently with a young woman, a family friend Ruth and I have known for some time, brought the importance of this message home to me in a new way. She was confused about her career, uncertain about a new relationship, and generally flailing away at life. She'd lost her zeal and didn't know what to do about it.

After reminding her of the importance of working out and getting her rest, I heard myself say, "You know, you're never going to be really fulfilled—you'll just be chasing fluff—until you make a decision to be a serious reader. Anybody who's not a reader has got to constantly be thinking up forms of amusement to keep themselves occupied. Think about it! You've got to line up your television programs, or figure out what you and your friends are going to do tonight—is it the dart tournament or Fantasy Football? If you're not a reader, your *entire* life is spent arranging those kinds of things to keep yourself occupied. There's nothing wrong with those things, but at the end of the day they really don't make much difference.

"To have a healthy body," I told her, "you've got to be eating chicken breasts and salmon, broccoli, and carrots—all those good foods. Suppose you ate nothing but ice cream, chocolate éclairs, and French fries all the time. They might taste good and fill your tummy, but after a while, your body is not going to *feel* good! By the same token, your brain needs broccoli, salmon, and carrots— and those are books!"

That day I issued her this challenge: "Ten percent of your income has got to be committed to your ongoing education—

books, tapes, seminars, and retreats. I want you to read one book a week for the next five weeks—but remember, you're only a world's leading authority if those five books are on the same subject. Read any five books you want, but at the end of each book," I told her, "I want a book report."

So today, with this book, Dr. Williams is applying a practical prescription. I can't meet with all of you—my office hours are jammed. But I'm offering you this same prescription, free of charge—no waiting rooms, no needles, no insurance hassles. I promise you that if you apply the medicine of books to your ailing life—wherever you are ailing—you'll see a noticeable improvement before you know it. Want to look and feel ten years younger? Books will do more for your appearance, believe it or not, than any makeover. They change you from the inside out— the kind of change that is deep, permanent, and powerful.

Thanks for reading this book. I hope it inspires you to read more, read often, read daily, and read to change your life. If this book has made a difference for you, I'd love to hear *your* book report.

In closing, I must concur with author Arnold Lobel, who wrote, "Books to the ceiling, books to the sky, my pile of books is a mile high. How I love them! How I need them! I'll have a long beard by the time I read them." May the same sentiment be true of you, my friends.

Bibliography

Books

Allender, Dan B., Ph.D. *To Be Told: Know Your Story, Shape Your Future.* Colorado Springs, CO: WaterBrook Press, 2006.

Bradbury, Ray. *Fahrenheit 451.* New York: Ballantine, 1953.

Corrigan, Maureen. *Leave Me Alone, I'm Reading: Finding Myself and Losing Myself in Books.* New York: Random House, 2005.

Edmundson, Mark. *Why Read?* New York: Bloomsbury USA, 2004.

Goodwin, Doris Kearns. *Team of Rivals: The Political Genius of Abraham Lincoln.* New York: Simon & Schuster, 2005.

Grant, George, and Karen Grant. *Shelf Life: How Books Have Changed the Destinies and Desires of Men and Nations.* Nashville, TN: Cumberland House Publishing, 1999.

Hayward, Steven F. *Greatness: Reagan, Churchill, and the Making of Extraordinary Leaders.* New York: Crown Forum, 2005.

Lengel, Edward G. *General George Washington: A Military Life.* New York: Random House, 2005.

Leveen, Steve. *The Little Guide to Your Well-Read Life: How to Get More Books in Your Life and More Life from Your Books.* Delray Beach, FL: Levenger Press, 2005.

Lombardo, John. *A Fire to Win: The Life and Times of Woody Hayes.* New York: Thomas Dunne Books, 2005.

McCormick, Blaine. *Ben Franklin: America's Original Entrepreneur.* Irvine, CA: Entrepreneur Press, 2005.

Menzer, Joe. *Buckeye Madness: The Glorious, Tumultuous, Behind-the-*

Scenes Story of Ohio State Football. New York: Simon & Schuster, 2005.

Stone, Dave, and Rick Rusaw. *60 Simple Secrets Every Pastor Should Know*. Loveland, CO: Group Publishing, 2002.

Trelease, Jim. *The Read-Aloud Handbook* (sixth edition). New York: Penguin, 2006.

Also: "James Madison: The Man Who Loved Books," an essay by Lynne Cheney.

Thanks to the following publications for contributing to this book:

> *Akron Beacon Journal*
> *Atlanta Journal-Constitution*
> *Family Circle*
> *New York Times*
> *O, The Oprah Magazine*
> *Orange County Register*
> *Orlando Sentinel*
> *Philadelphia Inquirer*
> *Publishers Weekly*
> *USA Today*
> *Wall Street Journal*

Resources

Books

To help fight illiteracy, contact the National Center for Family Literacy, www.famlit.org.

For adults who can't read, contact ProLiteracy Worldwide, www.pro literacy.org.

(Thanks to *PARADE* for providing these resources.)

Books that teach reading (suggested for teachers by a teacher—with thanks to Kelly Robertson):

Beers, Kylene. *When Kids Can't Read: What Teachers Can Do*. Portsmouth, NH: Heinemann, 2002.

Fountas, Irene C., and Gay Su Pinnell. *Guiding Readers and Writers: Teaching Comprehension, Genre, and Content Literacy*. Portsmouth, NH: Heinemann, 2000.

Harvey, Stephanie. *Nonfiction Matters: Reading, Writing, and Research in Grades 3–8*. Portland, ME: Stenhouse Publishers, 1998.

Harvey, Stephanie, and Anne Goudvis. *Strategies That Work: Teaching Comprehension to Enhance Understanding*. Portland, ME: Stenhouse Publishers, 2000.

Robb, Laura. *Teaching Reading in Middle School* (Grades 5 & Up). New York: Scholastic Professional Books, 2000.

Tovani, Cris. *I Read It, But I Don't Get It: Comprehension Strategies for Adolescent Readers*. Portland, ME: Stenhouse Publishers, 2000.

Reading Programs

Read to Achieve: An NBA-sponsored program, it is "a year-round campaign to help young people develop a lifelong love for reading and encourage adults to read regularly to children." Read to Achieve reaches an estimated 50 million children every year. For more on this outstanding program, visit www.nba.com/nba_cares/.

International Reading Association: www.reading.org

The Literacy Site: www.theliteracysite.com

National Endowment for the Arts The Big Read Program: www.neabigread.org

Reach Out and Read: www.reachoutandread.org/

Reading Resources for Parents

Children's Book Council: www.cbcbooks.org

Guys Read: www.guysread.com

PBS Parents: www.pbs.org/parents

Reading Is Fundamental: www.rif.org

Scholastic: www.scholastic.org

Websites for Trading Books

Bookins: www.bookins.com

Frugal Reader: www.FrugalReader.com

PaperBackSwap: www.PaperBackSwap.com

TitleTrader: www.TitleTrader.com

\Inclusion of these sites in this publication is not an endorsement, either by the authors or the publisher. They are offered simply as suggestions for other reading resources. We apologize in advance for any we may have missed.

For Further Information

You can contact Pat Williams at:

Pat Williams
c/o Orlando Magic
8701 Maitland Summit Boulevard
Orlando, FL 32810
phone: (407) 916-2404
pwilliams@orlandomagic.com

Visit Pat Williams's website at:
www.PatWilliamsMotivate.com

If you would like to set up a speaking engagement for Pat Williams, please call or write his assistant, Andrew Herdliska, at the above address or call him at (407) 916-2401. Requests can also be faxed to (407) 916-2986 or e-mailed to aherdliska@ orlandomagic.com.

We would love to hear from you. Please send your comments about this book to Pat Williams at the above address or in care of our publisher at the address below. Thank you.

Health Communications, Inc.
3201 S.W. 15th Street
Deerfield Beach, FL 33442
Fax: (954) 360-0034

Index